SEVEN POSTURES OF CHRIST

The front cover picture, *Summer Shadows in the Mournes,* is by David Bond Walker, RUA, 1891-1977. For many years he was an esteemed elder in the assembly at Newcastle, Co. Down, N. Ireland. Permission to use it has been granted by his twin daughters, Elizabeth and Margaret, who still live in Newcastle.

SEVEN POSTURES
OF CHRIST

Mervyn Wishart

RITCHIE
John Ritchie Publishing
40 Beansburn, Kilmarnock, Scotland

ISBN-13: 978 1 912522 62 0

Copyright © 2019 by John Ritchie Ltd.
40 Beansburn, Kilmarnock, Scotland

www.ritchiechristianmedia.co.uk

Typeset by John Ritchie Ltd., Kilmarnock
Printed by Bell & Bain Ltd., Glasgow

Contents

Foreword

The Gospel writers are careful to note the many different postures of the Lord Jesus on His earthly pathway. These not only portray an attitude of body, but also often depict a deeper and richer spiritual truth.

Mervyn Wishart in this book, *'Seven Postures of Christ'*, deals with a subject which hitherto has received but scant attention.

It first considers the Lord Jesus 'stooping' to write on the ground with His finger; a telling picture of His mighty stoop from Godhead glory into manhood.

Then follow postures portraying the reality of that manhood; revealing just how near He came to us to become our Saviour.

The closing scene is of the Lord 'bowing' His head upon the Cross; as if, in holy salutation, He acknowledges everything complete that He had come to do.

Every paragraph, saturated with Holy Scripture, engages our hearts with the Saviour.

Jack Strahan
Enniskillen
Co. Fermanagh
June 2019

As a reader of books over many years, I have a private list of those that have made a difference in my personal spiritual life, through touching my mind: they have illuminated the intelligence from Scripture, engaged the emotions with the Saviour, and then motivated the will to service for Him. This book will be added to that list – tonight.

When the manuscript was given to me I started to read, and I could not put it down until I reached the last page. Now I enjoy taking the book section by section, allowing familiar Scriptures to paint the Saviour in postures familiar but new, so that we are compelled to stop and allow the Spirit of God to lead us to worship.

The writing is plain and easily read; alliteration is useful and not over-used. Digressions are illuminative and helpful. I recommend this book highly.

Jim Allen
Newtownabbey
Co. Antrim
June 2019

Preface

The seed which encouraged me to write this little book was planted in my mind during a conversation with a long-time Christian friend, George Johnson. We met unexpectedly a few years ago in Portugal. We walked together and talked about a variety of Biblical subjects, one of which was the postures of the Lord Jesus during His life on earth.

George told me that one day, when he was travelling by plane from London to Belfast, the seat allocated to him was beside a well-known MP and minister of the gospel, who later became the First Minister of Northern Ireland. George knew Dr Ian Paisley very well; they had been friends for a long time, and soon they engaged in conversation. Dr Paisley was perusing some pages with great interest. When George enquired what he was studying, Dr Paisley replied that he was writing a book about the postures of Christ. I don't know if his book was ever finished, but if so it would doubtless have expanded on the subject much more eloquently than I have done.

So I meditated on the theme and the seed began to germinate. I would use little segments now and then, both in gospel preaching and in ministry, and about a year ago I began drawing the thoughts together. Everyone who desires to speak or write about the person of Christ will soon discover that they have embarked on a limitless task. Ephesians 3:8 speaks of the unsearchable riches of Christ, so the scanty thoughts expressed here could never do justice to the theme.

There is something that unites all true believers: they have a love for Christ. It may not be what it should be, nor what it could be, but each one can gladly use the words of the Apostle John, 'we love him, because he first loved us.' He has not only saved our souls but he has won our hearts. Thomas Kelly expresses the thought in his hymn, 'We'll sing of the Shepherd that died'— 'No subject's so glorious as He, no theme's so affecting to us.'

Every word He spoke, every place He visited, every step He took on His many journeys, every miracle He performed, every posture—every detail about Him given in Scripture is of immense interest to the Christian.

David, whose name means 'Beloved', attracted people to be with him. Even in the days of his rejection, when he was in the cave of Adullam, many gathered to him and he became a captain over them. They loved him for who he was in himself and because of how he had rescued them from the difficulties in which they were found: some were in debt, some in distress, some discontented. They loved him because he had gone down alone into the valley of Elah to face Goliath and win the victory for them. As they watched him go, they must have thought, 'He's taking my place; he's facing the enemy for me.' The first words of the New Testament introduce us to 'Jesus Christ, *the Son of David*' (Matt. 1:1). He could say, 'And I, if I be lifted up from the earth, will draw all men (all kinds of men) unto me' (John 12:32).

This book looks briefly at only some of the postures of Christ from the time of His birth until His ascension from the Mount of Olives. Readers will doubtless think of others; the study is not exhaustive, nor could it ever be.

Mervyn Wishart
Newcastle, Co. Down
June 2019

CHAPTER 1

Stooping Down

He stooped down (John 8:8)

Having spent the night on the Mount of Olives, the Lord Jesus came early in the morning to the temple and sat down to teach (vv. 1-2). His teaching was suddenly interrupted. A group of Jewish religious leaders, scribes and Pharisees, burst in, bringing a woman accused of adultery. Her accusers said that her guilt was established beyond doubt: 'She was taken in the very act.'

They set her 'in the midst' of the crowd who had gathered in the early morning to listen to the Lord Jesus. Then they quoted from the Old Testament the punishment to fit her crime: 'Moses in the law commanded us, that such should be stoned: but what sayest thou? This they said tempting him that they might have to accuse him' (vv. 5-6; Lev. 20:10).

Had the Lord said, 'She should be stoned', then He would have been charged with advocating that they should break the Roman law, for the Jews were forbidden to carry out capital punishment. Later they would acknowledge to Pilate, 'It is not lawful for us to put any man to death' (John 18:31). If He had said 'No, she should not be stoned,' then they would have charged Him with undermining the Law of Moses.

What would He do? How would He answer? 'But Jesus stooped down, and with his finger, wrote on the ground, as though he heard them not' (8:6). We are not told what the Lord wrote. Doubtless, had we needed to know, it would have been recorded. However, we are told where He wrote: He wrote on the ground, in the dust. Man was created from the dust of the ground (Gen. 2:7). In Psalm 103:14 David wrote, 'For he knoweth our frame: he remembereth that we are dust.' When they persisted in asking Him, He stood up and said, 'He that is without sin among you, let him first cast a stone at her.' Campbell Morgan said, 'That one sentence put me out of the stone throwing business for the rest of my life.' 'And again he stooped down and wrote on the ground.' He did not say that the woman should not be stoned, but His question was to her accusers, 'who among you is qualified to be her executioner?'

'Without sin'—the standard was high. This is the only time this particular phrase occurs in the New Testament. Who would measure up to such a standard? What a dramatic effect His words had on the band of accusers. 'And they which heard it, being convicted by their own conscience, went out one by one, beginning at the eldest, even unto the last: and Jesus was left alone, and the woman standing in the midst' (v. 9). The eldest left first, doubtless convicted of the many sins of a long lifetime. The youngest, though not so far advanced on life's journey, still had a conscience smitten with guilt, and they also left. As they made their exit, each person was admitting that they were unfit to carry out the sentence.

For the first time the Lord Jesus spoke to the woman. 'He

said unto her, Woman, where are those thine accusers? Hath no man condemned thee? She said, No man, Lord. [The only words that she spoke in the story.] And Jesus said unto her, Neither do I condemn thee: go, and sin no more' (vv. 10-11).

Notice how tenderly He addresses her as 'Woman', the name He used on more than one occasion when speaking to His mother. He, the only one who had the moral right to condemn her, said, 'Neither do I condemn thee: go, and sin no more.' He had not come to condemn, but to save (John 3:17). 'For the Law was given by Moses, but grace and truth came by Jesus Christ' (1:17). For this poor sinful woman, there was no condemnation.

How thankful every believer should be, 'There is therefore now no condemnation to them which are in Christ Jesus' (Romans 8:1). We see grace and truth in beautiful harmony working in perfect balance. The Lord in no way condoned her sin. He said, 'Go, and sin no more.' Also of note are the first words of the Lord when He resumed His teaching in the temple, 'Then spake Jesus again unto them, saying, I am the Light of the world: He that followeth me shall not walk in darkness, but shall have the light of life' (John 8:12).

We read twice in John 8 that He stooped down (vv. 6, 8). This was the One who left the heights of glory to stoop down: to be born in Bethlehem, live in Nazareth, preach in Galilee, teach in Jerusalem, and be crucified outside its city wall, for the glory of God, for the defeat of Satan, for the blessing of creation, and to make salvation available for mankind.

To understand something of His downward stoop, we must first consider the scenes of glory that He left. Isaiah speaks of 'the Lord sitting upon a throne, high and lifted up, and his train filled the temple' (6:1). The Lord Jesus could speak of 'the glory which I had with thee before the world was' (John 17:5). John commenced his Gospel with a declaration of the deity of Christ: 'In the beginning was the Word, and the Word was with God, and the Word was God. The same was in the beginning with God' (1:1-2). He could say to His disciples, 'Ye shall see the Son of Man ascend up where he was before' (6:62).

Secondly, to grasp something more of His downward stoop, we must remember the depths to which He descended. In one sublime sentence in Philippians 2:5-8, Paul covers the stoop of the Lord Jesus from the throne to the cross.

'Let this mind be in you, which was also in Christ Jesus' (v. 5). All doctrine has a practical implication for our lives. Reading a passage like this, brimming with rich devotional thoughts of our Lord, it is easy to overlook the message for us, 'Let this mind be in you . . .'

'Who, being in the form of God' (v. 6). This is in the imperfect tense, indicating indefinite continuance, past, present and future. He ever was, He is now, and He will ever be in the form of God. This includes the whole nature and essence of deity. He is 'Jesus Christ the same yesterday, and today, and forever' (Heb. 13:8). When He was born in Bethlehem, it was still true, 'Who, being in the form of God'; working as a carpenter in Nazareth, it was still true, 'Who, being in the form of God.'

'The Son of God could not possibly divest Himself of the form of God at His incarnation without thereby ceasing to be God' (E. H. Gifford). The disciples were able to say, 'We beheld his glory, the glory as of the only begotten of the Father, full of grace and truth' (John 1:14).

'[He] thought it not robbery to be equal with God' (v. 6). The expression means that He did not count equality with God something to be grasped after (because it was already His). The Serpent said to Adam and Eve that, if they should eat of the tree in the midst of the garden, 'Ye shall be as gods' (Gen. 3:5). Satan's aspiration for himself was, 'I will exalt my throne above the stars of God . . . I will be like the most High' (Isa. 14:13-14). What they aspired to, but never attained, the Lord Jesus eternally was.

'But made himself of no reputation' (v. 7). The expression indicates utter self-denial: He emptied Himself, His life was poured out in the service of others. He could say to His disciples, 'For even the Son of man came not to be ministered unto but to minister, and to give his life a ransom for many' (Mark 10:45), and 'I am among you as he that serveth' (Luke 22:27). At Calvary, Isaiah 53:12 was fulfilled: 'He hath poured out his soul unto death.'

'and took upon him the form of a servant' (v. 7). The angels' highest calling is to be the servants of God. 'And of the angels he saith, Who maketh his angels spirits, and his ministers a flame of fire . . . Are they not all ministering spirits, sent forth to minister for them who shall be heirs of salvation?' (Heb. 1:7, 14). They can rise no higher; their lot is servitude. In contrast, the Lord Jesus had to stoop down in order to become a servant. On earth He was God's perfect servant, there was no one to compare with Him. Jehovah said of Him, 'Behold my servant, whom I uphold; mine elect, in whom my soul delighteth' (Isa. 42:1). 'Never was the form of God more fully manifested on earth than in Him who wore the servant's form' (H. C. Hewlett).

Though in the very form of God,
With heavenly glory crowned,
Thou didst partake of human flesh,
Beset with sorrow round.

Joseph Stennett

'and was made in the likeness of men' (v. 7). These words do not detract from His true manhood. The statement guards the essential fact that He was not only man, but God. 'Made in the likeness of men' (plural) emphasizes His link with the race of mankind. 'Forasmuch then, as the children are partakers of flesh and blood, he also himself likewise took part of the same' (Heb. 2:14). In becoming man, the Lord Jesus became 'lower than the angels' (v. 9). 'For verily he took not on him the nature of angels; but he took on him the seed of Abraham' (v. 16).

Verily God, yet become truly human —
Lower than angels to die in our stead;
How hast Thou, long promised Seed of the woman,
Trod on the serpent and bruised his head!

H. d'A. Champney

'And being found in fashion as a man . . .' (v. 8). This refers to His outward appearance. Though sinless, He shared human experience. He was weary, He slept, He was hungry, He was thirsty, He wept. The woman of Samaria said to her neighbours, 'Come, see a man . . .' (John 4:29). The blind man who received his sight gave a clear testimony of his meeting with Christ: 'A man that is called Jesus made clay and anointed my eyes' (9:11).

'he humbled himself' (v. 8). Every downward step of His condescension was a voluntary act. He could say, 'I am meek and lowly in heart' (Matt. 11:29).

'and became obedient unto death' (v. 8). His obedience to God His Father was to the point of death. His first recorded words were, 'I must be about my Father's business.' His words spoken on the evening before He was crucified were, 'I have glorified thee on the earth: I have finished the work which thou gavest me to do.' As the last Adam, He stands in stark contrast with the first Adam. 'For as by one man's disobedience many were made sinners, so by the obedience of one shall many be made righteous' (Rom. 5:19).

'even the death of the cross' (v. 8). With this statement Paul has reached the lowest point of the Saviour's humiliation. He had been set at nought by Herod and his men of war, falsely accused, blindfolded and buffeted in the house of Caiaphas, crowned with thorns and scourged in Pilate's judgment hall. From there He went through the narrow streets of Jerusalem, carrying His cross, out through the city gate and onwards towards Golgotha. With our limited appreciation, we say with Paul, 'even the death of the cross.'

The conjunctions (joining words) in these verses are worthy of note. There are five within this one sentence. Verse 7: 'but', 'and' (twice). Verse 8: 'and' (twice). These are used to convey the thought of a downward stoop, culminating at the cross. The lowest point is spoken of in Psalm 22:15, 'Thou hast brought me into the dust of death.'

> *And did the holy and the just,*
> *The sovereign of the skies,*
> *Stoop down to wretchedness and dust,*
> *That guilty worms might rise?*
> Anne Steele

Out of the ivory palaces,
Into a world of woe,
Only His great eternal love
Made my Saviour go.
Henry Barraclough

CHAPTER 2

Lying

'Mark the place where he shall lie' (Ruth 3:4).

At least four times in the New Testament we read of the Lord Jesus lying.

1. Lying in the manger: His poverty

   'And she brought forth her firstborn son, and wrapped him in swaddling clothes, and laid him in a manger' (Luke 2:7).

2. Lying in the ship: His peace

   'And he was in the hinder part of the ship, asleep on a pillow' (Mark 4:38).

3. Lying on the ground: His prostration

   'And he went a little farther, and fell on his face, and prayed' (Matt 26:39).

4. Lying in the tomb: His place of burial

   'And the women also, which came with him from Galilee, followed after, and beheld the sepulchre, and how his body was laid' (Luke 23:55).

1. Lying in the manger: His poverty

In the Old Testament there are three references to a feeding trough for animals where the word *crib* is used: Job 39:9, Proverbs 14:4, and Isaiah 1:3— 'The ox knoweth his owner, and the ass his master's crib…'.

In the New Testament there are three references where the word *manger* is used: Luke 2:7, 12, 16. The manger was made of wood by a carpenter. Little did the man who made it realize that this manger would one day be used as a cradle. Never in his wildest imagination did he envisage that the incarnate Son of God, the Creator of all things, would one day be laid in that manger by the tender hands of His young mother, Mary.

In the circumstances in which Mary found herself she did the very best she could do to make the child as safe, warm and comfortable as possible; '[she] wrapped him in swaddling clothes, and laid him in a manger' (Luke 2:7). 'All things were made by him' (John 1:3)—now He lay in a roughly constructed wooden manger made by a carpenter from Bethlehem.

The sign to the shepherds

The message brought to them by the angelic messenger was: 'And this shall be a sign unto you; Ye shall find the babe wrapped in swaddling clothes, *lying in a manger*' (Luke 2:12). Immediately after the sign was given, we are told: 'And suddenly there was with the angel a multitude of the heavenly host praising God, and saying, Glory to God in the highest, and on earth peace, good will toward men' (vv. 13-14). There may well have been other babies born in Bethlehem that night, but only one was laid in a manger. The shepherds were therefore assured that this was the child of whom the angel had spoken (v. 16).

The sign to Israel

'Therefore the Lord himself shall give you a sign; Behold, *a virgin shall conceive*, and bear a son, and shall call his name Immanuel' (Isa. 7:14). The angel who appeared to Joseph confirmed this majestic truth when he said, '. . . that which is conceived in her is of the Holy Ghost,' and then Matthew quotes from Isaiah, 'Behold a virgin shall be with child, and shall bring forth a son, and they shall call his name Emmanuel, which being interpreted is, God with us' (Matt. 1:20-23).

In summary, the child cradled in a manger was a sign to the shepherds, and the Messiah born of a virgin was a sign to Israel. As we view this humble scene at Bethlehem, may we remember the words of Ruth 3:4 and mark the place where He lay.

After eight days Mary and Joseph brought the child up to the temple. How beautiful are the words, 'they brought him to Jerusalem, to present him to the Lord' (Luke 2:22). The offering that Mary brought for her purification was a further indication of poverty: 'A pair of turtledoves, or two young pigeons' (v. 24). This was the acceptable offering when a lamb could not be brought: 'And if she be not able to bring a lamb, then she shall bring two turtledoves, or two young pigeons' (Lev. 12:8). As we think of the humble circumstances into which the Lord Jesus was born, we do well to remember that it was '. . . for your sakes he became poor' (2 Cor. 8:9).

> *Lo, within a manger lies*
> *He who built the starry skies;*
> *He who, throned in height sublime,*
> *Sits amid the cherubim.*
>   Edward Caswall

2. Lying in the ship: His peace

After a busy day teaching the multitude by the seaside, in the evening the Lord said to His disciples, 'Let us pass over unto the other side' (Mark 4:35). So they embarked on a journey across the Sea of Galilee travelling towards the country of the Gadarenes. 'And there arose a great storm of wind, and the waves beat into the ship, so that it was now full' (v. 37). The ship and all on board now appeared to be in great peril.

It is at this point that we are told, 'And he was in the hinder part of the ship, asleep on a pillow' (v. 38). We see how the Lord Jesus made good use of every moment of His time. After a busy day He sleeps while travelling, thus conserving His energy. He knew that immediately they arrived at their destination busy service would resume, and He would meet the man with an unclean spirit, who lived among the tombs (5:2).

We can see a marked contrast between this passage and Jonah chapter 1, where we also read of a ship in great peril. 'But the Lord sent out a great wind into the sea, so that the ship was like to be broken . . . But Jonah was gone down into the sides of the ship; and he lay, and was fast asleep' (vv. 4-5).

The Lord Jesus was the perfect servant of Jehovah. He never once deviated from the path of the divine will. However, Jonah had embarked on a path of self will and independence: he had disobeyed the clear instruction from the Lord that he should go to Nineveh. His sleep was a sleep of carelessness. He was content, even though he was in the wrong place, going in the wrong direction. No other servant can be compared to Christ: they can only be contrasted with Him.

The peace which the Lord Jesus enjoyed every moment, He

bequeathed to His disciples: 'Peace I leave with you, my peace I give unto you: . . . Let not your heart be troubled, neither let it be afraid' (John 14:27). He had perfect control of the elements and had no cause to fear them. He controls the wind and commands it to do His bidding: 'The Lord hath his way in the whirlwind and in the storm, and the clouds are the dust of his feet' (Nahum 1:3). He also controls the force of the wind: 'For he looketh to the ends of the earth . . . To make the weight for the winds' (Job 28:24-25).

The weather forecasters may be able to predict the direction and strength of the wind with some accuracy, but they can do absolutely nothing to change its course or strength: 'The wind bloweth where it listeth' (John 3:8). But we read of the Lord Jesus, 'And he arose, and rebuked the wind, and said to the sea, Peace, be still. And the wind ceased, and there was a great calm' (Mark 4:39). No wonder the disciples were amazed, 'and said one to another, What manner of man is this, that even the wind and the sea obey him?' (v. 41). In Jonah we read, 'But the Lord sent out a great wind . . . God prepared a vehement east wind' (1:4; 4:8). How reassuring it is for us to remember that our God is in perfect control of the elements and God's weather is never at variance with God's work.

3. Lying on the ground: His prostration

A reading of the three synoptic Gospels gives us a description of our Lord's progressive postures in prayer in the garden of Gethsemane.

Luke records that the Lord Jesus moved a short distance away from His disciples: 'And he was withdrawn from them about a stone's cast, and *kneeled down*, and prayed' (22:41).

Mark states: 'And he went forward a little, and *fell on the ground*, and prayed' (14:35).

Matthew adds: 'He went a little farther, and *fell on his face*, and prayed' (26:39).

In Matthew 26 the Lord is prostrate on the ground, His face pressing the dust of earth. In Genesis 3:17 we read 'cursed is the ground'. He was the One who had come to ultimately remove the curse and restore a fallen creation and bring salvation within the reach of all, but at such a cost.

In contrast, John speaks not of the Lord falling down, but of others falling down before Him: 'As soon then as he had said unto them, *I am he*, they went backward, and fell to the ground' (18:6).

Matthew speaks of 'a great multitude with swords and staves' (26:47), and John adds 'lanterns and torches and weapons' (18:3). The great multitude was caused to go backward involuntarily and fall forward before the great I AM.[1] This is a picture in miniature of a future day when, 'at the name of Jesus every knee should bow . . . and every tongue should confess that Jesus Christ is Lord, to the glory of God the Father' (Phil. 2:10-11).

His Submission

It was foretold in prophecy: 'Sacrifice and offering thou didst not desire . . . Then said I, Lo, I come: in the volume of the book it is written of me, I delight to do thy will, O my God: yea, thy law is within my heart' (Ps. 40:6-8).

---

[1]See Exodus 3:13-14; John 6:35; 9:5: 10:9, 11; 11:25; 14:6; 15:1.

The course of His life was marked by an unswerving determination to do the will of God— 'And he that sent me is with me: the Father hath not left me alone; for I do always those things that please him' (John 8:29). His submission to the Father's will continued to the end. 'He humbled himself, and became obedient unto death, even the death of the cross' (Phil. 2:8).

In Gethsemane His submission to His Father's will was absolute and final. He prayed, 'O my Father, if it be possible, let this cup pass from me: nevertheless not as I will, but as thou wilt' (Matt. 26:39).

The Fall of man in the garden of Eden was the result of disobedience. Now the Lord Jesus, by an act of obedience, will bring salvation within the reach of all. Paul explains the wonder of God's plan: 'For as by one man's disobedience many were made sinners, so by the obedience of one shall many be made righteous' (Rom. 5:19).

His Solitude

All of the disciples with the exception of Judas, were with the Lord in the garden. From the group of eleven, He took with Him Peter and the two sons of Zebedee. It was to the three that He made the request, 'Tarry ye here and watch with me' (Matt. 26:38).

Three times the Lord returned to find the three of them sleeping and He said to Peter, 'What, could ye not watch with me one hour?' (26:40). As the Lord endured the unparalleled anguish and sorrow of Gethsemane, He was alone.

He went a little farther all alone,
Into the darkest night this world has known.
The olive trees their silent vigil kept;
Disciples slept.

He went a little farther to a tree
That stretched its cruel arms o'er Calvary.
No other could have suffered in the stead
Of Him who bled.

He went a little farther: Christ arose,
And in His grave left all our vanquished foes.
And now in Heaven He lives to intercede
For all our need.

His Sorrow

The proceedings in the upper room had concluded with the singing of a hymn (Matt. 26:30). After His arrival in the garden, 'he began to be sorrowful and very heavy [troubled] (v. 37). He said to the three disciples, 'My soul is exceeding sorrowful [full of grief, JND], even unto death' (v. 38; Mark 14:34). No sorrow could ever compare with His sorrow: 'behold, and see if there be any sorrow like unto my sorrow, which is done unto me' (Lam. 1:12).

The Lord spoke of His sorrow as, 'even unto death'. The anticipation of the cross was now the cause of His grief: 'Jesus therefore, knowing all things that should come upon him, went forth' (John 18:4). Truly He was 'a man of sorrows, and acquainted with grief' (Isa. 53:3).

When Benjamin, the youngest son of Jacob, was born, his

mother Rachel called him *Benoni*, 'son of my sorrow': but his father named him *Benjamin*, 'the son of the right hand' (Gen. 35:18). Doubtless we can see in this verse 'things concerning Himself'. Our Lord Jesus was both the 'Son of sorrow', and the 'Son of the right hand'. He experienced the unparalleled sorrow of Calvary, and He now fills the unrivalled place of glory at the right hand of God (Heb. 1:3).

> *'Man of sorrows,' what a name*
> *For the Son of God who came*
> *Ruined sinners to reclaim!*
> *Hallelujah! what a Saviour.*
>   Philip P. Bliss

His Sweat

'And being in an agony he prayed more earnestly: and his sweat was as it were great drops of blood falling down to the ground' (Luke 22:44).

Sweat is mentioned three times in the Scriptures. The first concerned the curse which God had put upon the ground: 'cursed is the ground for thy sake' (Gen. 3:17). 'In the sweat of thy face shalt thou eat bread' (v. 19). The second is when the priests were forbidden to wear anything which caused them to sweat. When they were occupied in their priestly work, they were to avoid anything that came as a result of the Fall— 'they shall not gird themselves with any thing that causeth sweat' (Ezek. 44:18). The final mention is by Luke, concerning the One who came to ultimately remove every trace of the Fall, and in doing so He Himself undertook to bear both its results and its penalty. It emphasizes for us the intensity of His agony in prayer, and our hearts might well exclaim in wonder:

Gethsemane can I forget,
Or there Thy conflict see;
Thine agony and blood like sweat,
And not remember thee?

James Montgomery

His Sonship

The Lord's prayer in the garden was addressed to His Father (Matt. 26:39, 42). Mark records, 'And he said, Abba, Father, all things are possible unto thee; take away this cup from me: nevertheless not what I will, but what thou wilt). How amazing that the One who lay prostrate on the ground in an agony of soul, experiencing sorrow that no mortal ever knew, was the incarnate Son of God.

His Supplication

Luke emphasizes the intensity of His prayer in words that are beyond our understanding: 'And being in an agony he prayed more earnestly' (22:44). Matthew informs us that His prayer was repeated three times: 'saying the same words' (26:44). Hebrews adds yet more detail for us: 'Who in the days of his flesh, when he had offered up prayers and supplications with strong crying and tears unto him that was able to save him from death, and was heard in that he feared' (5:7). This verse may not refer exclusively to Gethsemane, but it certainly includes it.

Here is One who prayed as no other to the God who was able to answer; nevertheless, He accepted the will of God.

> *Was it for me He wept and prayed,*
> *When prostrate in the garden laid:*
> *That night within Gethsemane,*
> *Was it for me that agony?*
>
> John M. Whyte

His Strengthening

'And there appeared an angel unto him from heaven, strengthening him' (Luke 22:43). How amazing that the omnipotent God manifest in flesh should be strengthened by an angel. It should be noted that He had already expressed His submission to the Father's will: 'nevertheless not my will, but thine, be done' (v. 42). After His temptation in the wilderness, the victory having already been won and the devil put to flight, we read, 'Then the devil leaveth him, and, behold, angels came and ministered unto him' (Matt. 4:11).

4. Lying in the tomb: His place of burial

'And the women also, which came with him from Galilee, followed after, and beheld the sepulchre, and how *his body was laid*' (Luke 23:55).

Death by crucifixion was a method of capital punishment used by the Romans. It was reserved for the very worst criminals and very seldom used for Roman citizens. When Psalm 22 was written, around 1000 years BC, the writer could not possibly have envisaged that the Romans would occupy Jerusalem at the time of Christ and that He would be crucified outside the city. The graphic description is given in Psalm 22:16: 'They pierced my hands and my feet.' Speaking of a time yet future, Zechariah wrote: 'And one shall say unto him, What are these wounds in thine hands?' (13:6).

In contrast to the death of Christ, Scripture states clearly that His burial would be 'as the manner of the Jews is to bury' (John 19:40). It is an amazing fact that two of the most prominent Jews in Jerusalem, Joseph of Arimathaea and Nicodemus, came forward to work together to prepare His body for burial. There were not two more qualified men to see to it that Jewish customs were observed.

Matthew tells us that Joseph was 'a rich man' (27:57). Mark mentions his political influence, 'an honourable councillor' (15:43 JND). Luke speaks about his character, 'a good man, and a just' (23:50). John speaks of the allegiance he had to Christ, 'a [secret] disciple' (19:38). He was a member of the Sanhedrin, the inner circle of the Jewish council in Jerusalem; but '[he] had not consented unto the counsel and deed of them' (Luke 23:51).

Nicodemus 'first came to Jesus by night' (John 19:39). The question the Lord Jesus put to him was: 'Are you the teacher of Israel, and do not know these things?' (3:10 NKJV). Nicodemus was also a member of the Sanhedrin. He had voiced his objection in relation to their attitude to Christ: 'Doth our law judge any man, before it hear him, and know what he doeth?' (7:50-51).

After the Lord Jesus had died on the cross, we read: 'When the even was come, there came a rich man of Arimathaea, named Joseph, who also himself was Jesus' disciple: He went to Pilate, and begged the body of Jesus' (Matt. 27:57-58). Mark adds: 'And Pilate marvelled if he were already dead: and calling unto him the centurion, he asked him whether he had been any while dead. And when he knew it of the centurion, he gave the body to Joseph' (15:44-45).

Joseph, assisted by Nicodemus, tenderly withdrew the nails from His hands and feet and the crown of thorns from His head, and together they lowered His body to the ground and began the task of preparing it for burial.

> *Gently they took Him down,*
> *Unfixed His hands and feet;*
> *Took from His head the thorny crown,*
> *Brought forth the winding sheet.*
>
> *Fine linen, fitly made,*
> *Wrapped they around His face;*
> *Where never man before was laid*
> *Made they His resting place.*
>
> *Spices most sweet they brought,*
> *Aloes they brought and myrrh.*
> *Wound Him with these in linen clothes;*
> *Gave Him a sepulchre.*
>
> *Laid Him in hewn rock,*
> *Rolled to the door the stone;*
> *Watched the world add its waxen lock,*
> *And left Him there alone.*
>
> I. Y. Ewan, 'Last Touches'

There is a clear record given as to what both Joseph and Nicodemus contributed. Joseph donated his own new tomb, which he had hewn out of a rock (Matt. 27:60). He also bought fine linen (Mark 15:46). Matthew stresses that it was 'clean linen' (27:59). Nicodemus brought a mixture of myrrh and aloes, 'about an hundred pound weight' (John 19:39). They took the body of Jesus, and wound it in linen clothes with the spices, 'as the manner of the Jews is to bury' (19:40).

There was only a small number that followed Joseph and Nicodemus as they made their way to the sepulchre in the garden. 'And the women also, which came with him from Galilee, followed after, and beheld the sepulchre, and how his body was laid' (Luke 23:55). Mary Magdalene took special note of the location of the tomb, as she intended after the Sabbath to return early to anoint the Lord's body. 'And Mary Magdalene and Mary the mother of Joses beheld where he was laid' (Mark 15:47).

The tomb of a rich man

The sepulchre belonged to a rich man, Joseph of Arimathaea. Those who gave Him a cross outside the city gate would have thrown His body into a criminal's grave, but God intervened. His suffering, shame and humiliation are at an end, and God saw to it that His body lay in a rich man's tomb. This was in fulfilment of Isaiah 53:9: '[He was] with the rich in his death.'

> *Never more shall God, Jehovah,*
> *Smite the Shepherd with the sword.*
> *Ne'er again shall cruel sinners*
> *Set at nought our glorious Lord.*
> Robert C. Chapman

A new tomb

'Now in the place where he was crucified there was a garden; and in the garden a new sepulchre, wherein was never man yet laid' (John 19:41). It answers to the 'clean place' of Leviticus 6:11. Had a dead body previously occupied the tomb, it would have been rendered an unclean place (Num. 19:13).

When Elisha died and was buried, a short time later the Moabites invaded the land. There was a funeral taking place when they spied a band of men approaching. '. . . and they cast the man into the sepulchre of Elisha: and when the man was let down, and touched the bones of Elisha, he revived and stood up on his feet' (2 Kgs. 13:21).

The Lord Jesus was laid in a new tomb. There could be no claim that His resurrection could be attributed to another person. He arose by His own triumphant power. He said: 'Destroy this temple, and in three days I will raise it up' (John 2:19).

A garden tomb

'Now in the place where he was crucified there was a garden; and in the garden a new sepulchre' (John 19:41). The Bible begins with an account of the first garden: 'And the Lord God planted a garden eastward in Eden' (Gen. 2:8). The sad story of Eden was of defeat and the entrance of sin into the world with its devastating consequences for generations to come. In contrast, the victory was won at Calvary by 'the last Adam' (1 Cor. 15:45); and this garden would be the place where His resurrection from among the dead would be announced by the heavenly messengers: 'Fear not ye: for I know that ye seek Jesus, which was crucified. He is not here: for he is risen, as he said. Come, see the place where the Lord lay' (Matt 28:5-6).

The sepulchre was in a fragrant place, a garden. Inside, the tomb also bore the fragrance of the myrrh and aloes used by Joseph and Nicodemus to anoint His body. This was the only tomb never to bear the odour of corruption: 'But he, whom God raised again, saw no corruption' (Acts 13:37). We remind our hearts that He was the One of whom we read, 'All thy garments smell of myrrh, and aloes, and cassia, out of the ivory palaces' (Ps. 45:8). He brought to this sinful world something of the fragrance of heaven.

A rock hewn tomb

'And laid him in a sepulchre which was hewn out of a rock' (Mark 15:46). The construction of the sepulchre took many hours of hard work. No pneumatic tools or explosives were available: the labour intensive task would greatly increase the cost of providing the tomb. The result was a tomb probably the size of a small room, usually with a ledge on which to lay the body.

Because of the method of its construction it was clear that there was one way in and one way out. There was no possibility of a secret passage through which the disciples could have removed the body. How fitting that the One who is 'the Rock of Ages' (Isa. 26:4 JND margin) should be laid within the rock hewn tomb.

A guarded tomb

Inside the tomb there were 'two angels in white sitting, the one at the head, and the other at the feet, where the body of Jesus had lain' (John 20:12). Immediately after the burial of the Lord Jesus, 'the chief priests and Pharisees came together unto Pilate, Saying, Sir, we remember that that deceiver said, while he was yet alive, After three days I will rise again. Command therefore that the sepulchre be made sure until the third day, lest the disciples come by night and steal him away and say unto the people, He is risen from the dead: … Pilate said unto them, Ye have a watch: go your way, make it as sure as ye can.

So they went, and made the sepulchre sure, sealing the stone and setting a watch' (Matt. 27:64-66). Heaven's guard was inside the tomb; the Roman soldiers were on guard outside the tomb.

A sealed tomb

Matthew records that before Joseph left the tomb following the burial of Christ he rolled a great stone to the door of the sepulchre and departed. The stone is described by Mark as 'a very great stone' (16:4). In addition to the stone there was a seal; the seal secured the stone. To remove the stone and enter the tomb the seal must be broken. The three woman recorded by Mark came to the tomb early in the morning. They talked among themselves on the journey. Their concern was, 'Who shall roll us away the stone from the door of the sepulchre?'.

At the entrance to the den of lions in which Daniel was imprisoned, there was a stone and a seal bearing the King's signet. 'And a stone was brought, and laid upon the mouth of the den; and the king sealed it with his own signet, and the signet of his lords; that the purpose might not be changed concerning Daniel' (6:17).

It was the intention of those who sealed the tomb of the Lord Jesus that the purpose might never be changed: that Christ would remain in the tomb. However, 'the angel of the Lord descended from heaven, and came and rolled back the stone from the door, and sat upon it' (Matt. 28:2). The angel represented a higher authority than that of Rome. Not only did he break the seal and remove the stone, but in defiance of the power of Rome he sat upon it.

It has often been said: the stone was not rolled away to let the Lord Jesus out, but to let us look in and see that the tomb is empty.

A borrowed tomb

The one who preached in a borrowed boat, and rode on a borrowed donkey, and used a borrowed coin, lay in a borrowed tomb.

An empty tomb

When the women came early to the sepulchre, Luke records, 'And they found the stone rolled away from the sepulchre. And they entered in, and found not the body of the Lord Jesus' (24:2-3).

> *Vainly they watch His bed,*
> *Jesus my Saviour;*
> *Vainly they seal the dead,*
> *Jesus my Lord.*
>
> *Up from the grave He arose,*
> *With a mighty triumph o'er His foes.*
> Robert Lowry

CHAPTER 3

Sitting

1. Sitting in the midst of the doctors: asking questions

'And it came to pass, that after three days they found him in the temple, sitting in the midst of the doctors, both hearing them, and asking them questions. And all that heard him were astonished at his understanding and answers' (Luke 2:46-47).

The Lord Jesus was now twelve years old. Verse 40 states that He was 'filled with wisdom,' and verse 52, 'Jesus increased in wisdom.' What remarkable statements to consider! Only of the One who is God manifest in flesh could both statements be true. It fills our hearts with wonder to read of One who was 'filled with wisdom', and yet 'increased in wisdom.'

These doctors would have been men of learning, well versed in the Old Testament Scriptures; of the same ilk as Nicodemus in John chapter 3. Let us not miss the beauty of the two statements: He was 'in the temple,' and 'in the midst.' We are told that 'in his temple doth every [thing] speak of his glory' (Ps. 29:9). The one of whom every part of the temple speaks was now present, and the glory of His wisdom was evident to all who heard Him. Initially He listened on the periphery of the group, but soon He was invited to take His place in the midst.

This is one of a number of such references in Scripture to the Lord Jesus being in the midst. At Calvary, John records, '. . . where they crucified him, and two other with him, on either side one, and Jesus in the midst' (19:18). After His resurrection, 'Then the same day at evening, being the first day of the week . . . came Jesus and stood in the midst' (20:19, 26). The same words are used concerning another meeting in the upper room eight days later. 'Jesus . . . stood in the midst' (v. 26). John speaks of the Lord Jesus in His exaltation, 'And I beheld, and lo, in the midst of the throne. . . stood a Lamb as it had been slain' (Rev. 5:6). How precious to remember the reference in Matthew 18:20, 'For where two or three are gathered together in my name, there am I in the midst of them.' We read of this same glorious person walking in the midst of the seven golden candlesticks (Rev. 2:1).

The centrality of Christ on each of these occasions is a heart-warming study. The learned doctors must have wondered that one so young should be interested in listening to their conversation. They would have spoken of many Scriptures and many subjects. That's how it began: they were speaking and the Lord Jesus was listening. Then Luke continues to tell us that not only was He listening but He began to ask them questions. We are not told what His questions were, but whatever they were they caused the doctors of the law to be astonished at His understanding. Their interest was aroused to such a degree that they did what would previously have been considered unthinkable: they started to ask a twelve-year-old boy questions, inviting answers from Him.

Once again, the text informs us that they were astonished at His answers. Little did they know that the young boy in their midst was the one of whom they had often read 'there is no searching of his understanding' (Isa. 40:28). Many people would have been gathered within earshot to hear the words of wisdom from the sages as they conversed together. They too were astonished, for the text speaks of the fact that 'all that heard him were astonished' (Luke 2:47). When Mary and Joseph found Him in the temple 'they were amazed' (v. 48).

Our hearts are filled with wonder as we contemplate the scene and recall the words, 'his name shall be called Wonderful, Counsellor, . . .' (Isa. 9:6).

2. *Sitting on the well: revealing secrets*

'Jesus therefore, being wearied with his journey, sat thus on the well' (John 4:6).

This place is of great significance. The well had been dug by Jacob on a parcel of ground which he purchased from the children of Hamor, as recorded in Genesis 33:18-19, 'And Jacob came to Shalem, a city of Shechem . . . and he bought a parcel of a field . . . of the children of Hamor.'

Jacob later gave the land to his son Joseph (John 4:5). Ultimately, many years later, after the children of Israel carried Joseph's bones for forty years on their wilderness journeys, they buried them in this parcel of land. 'And the bones of Joseph, which the children of Israel brought up out of Egypt, buried they in Shechem, in a parcel of ground which Jacob bought of the sons of Hamor . . . for an hundred pieces of silver: and it became the inheritance of the children of Joseph' (Jos. 24:32). The land which was given by Jacob to Joseph had been purchased for one hundred pieces of silver. Now the Lord Jesus would speak to the Samaritan women about an infinitely greater gift: living water, purchased at infinite cost.

It is certainly a mark of the true humanity of Christ that He was wearied with His journey. Isaiah speaks of 'the everlasting God, the Lord, the Creator of the ends of the earth, fainteth not, neither is weary' (40:28). But as a man on earth we read that He was hungry (Mark 11:12); He was thirsty (John 19:28); He slept (Mark 4:38); He wept (John 11:35).

We must, of course, keep His deity always before us: 'The word was God' (John 1:1). Not setting aside what He ever was, the One who sat on Sychar's well that day was in a body of perfect, but real humanity.

'He left Judaea, and departed again into Galilee. And he must needs go through Samaria' (4:3-4). Israel at that time was divided into three main areas: Judaea in the south, Galilee in the north, and Samaria in between. Jewish travellers going north would often take a longer route to avoid the Samaritans, with whom they had no dealings (4:9). The Lord Jesus did not make the normal detour, which would have avoided Samaria, and that for a very good reason. It was to meet with one sinful Samaritan women so that she might know the joy of drinking of the water of life—the present experience of God's salvation.

He who preached to multitudes now speaks to one person, and as He spoke she listened. As He patiently responded to her three questions (vv. 9, 11-12), she had a growing appreciation of Him. At first, as she approached from a distance, she would have seen the figure of a man seated on the well. She recognized from His clothing that He was a Jew, and when she spoke to Him for a short time she said, 'Sir, I perceive that thou art a prophet.'

Her testimony later to the men of Samaria was, 'Come, see a man, which told me all things that ever I did: Is not this the

Christ?' In his Epistle, John makes the matter crystal clear: 'Whosoever believeth that Jesus is the Christ is born of God' (1 John 5:1). Our presentation of the gospel should lead those who listen to an appreciation both of who Christ is and what He has done. This woman saw Him as a man, a Jew, a prophet, the Christ; and after her testimony the men of Samaria added 'the Saviour of the World' (John 4:42).

We note the significance of the fact that the Lord went to Samaria. The valley of Achor, with its solemn association with the judgment of Achan (Jos. 7), stretched northward from beyond Jericho into Samaria. In Hosea 2:15 the prophet speaks of 'the valley of Achor for *a door of hope.*' In John 4:39 we read, 'many of the Samaritans of that city believed on him.' At their request, the Lord spent a further two days in the city, and 'many more believed because of his own word.'

The 'door of hope', which was opened to the Samaritans in John 4, is seen again in Acts 8. Philip preached Christ to them, 'And the people with one accord gave heed. And there was great joy in that city' (see vv. 5-8). The great commission given by the Lord was, 'Ye shall be witnesses unto me both in Jerusalem, and in all Judaea, and in Samaria, and unto the uttermost part of the earth' (Acts 1:8). The door of hope was surely opened to the Samaritans.

3. *Sitting on the Mount of Beatitudes: teaching*

After standing for the public reading of Scripture, the Lord gave the book to the minister, and sat down (Luke 4:20). At that point, 'the eyes of all them that were in the synagogue were fastened on him.' Then He said, 'This day is this scripture fulfilled in your ears' (v. 21).

In each of the four Gospels we have a record of the Lord teaching while He was seated.

Matthew chapters 5-7, The Sermon on the Mount: 'And seeing the multitudes, he went up into a mountain: and when he was set, his disciples came unto him; And he opened his mouth, and taught them, saying . . .' (5:1-2).

Mark 9:35-50, Teaching in the house at Capernaum: 'And he sat down, and called the twelve, and saith unto them . . .' (v. 35).

Luke 5:1-3, Teaching from the ship at Gennesaret: 'And he entered into one of the ships, which was Simon's, and prayed him that he would thrust out a little from the land. And he sat down, and taught the people out of the ship' (v. 3).

John 8:2-59, Teaching in the temple at Jerusalem: 'And early in the morning he came again into the temple, and all the people came unto him; and he sat down, and taught them' (v. 2); 'but Jesus hid himself, and went out of the temple . . .' (v. 59).

What made the teaching of our Lord Jesus unique?

He spoke with authority:

'. . . the people were astonished at his doctrine; For he taught them as one having authority, and not as the scribes' (Matt. 7:28-29). His words carried all the authority of the triune God. He alone could say 'My doctrine is not mine, but his that sent me' (John 7:16).

He spoke with veracity, yet with grace:

Every word was truth in the absolute sense. He said 'I am

the truth' (Jn. 14:6). John writes of Him as 'the faithful and true witness' (Rev. 3:14). While His teaching was truth, it was ministered with grace: 'grace and truth came by Jesus Christ' (John 1:17). The people marvelled at 'the gracious words which proceeded out of his mouth' (Luke 4:22).

He spoke with vitality:

'It is the spirit that quickeneth . . . the words that I speak unto you, they are spirit, and they are life' (John 6:63); 'His word was with power' (Luke 4:32).

He spoke with consistency:

His actions were ever and always in harmony with His teaching. Luke speaks of '. . . all that Jesus began both to do and to teach, until the day in which he was taken up' (Acts 1:1-2). Paul writes, 'as the truth is in Jesus' (Eph. 4:21). We are called to follow not only what He said, but what He was, and what He did. In whatever way we consider it, His teaching was beyond compare, 'Never man spake like this man' (John 7:46).

His authority was absolute: no higher authority than the triune God. His veracity was absolute: The word of the 'God that cannot lie' (Titus 1:2). The vitality and power of His words were absolute: no demon, no disease, no storm, no mountainous seas, not even death, could withstand His words. The consistency of His perfect life was absolute: No one else could claim 'He that hath sent me is with me: the Father hath not left me alone; for I do always those things that please him' (John 8:29).

4. Sitting on a donkey: entering Jerusalem

In preparation for the journey to Jerusalem, the Lord sent two of His disciples to a nearby village, where He told them they would find a donkey tied and a colt with her. Their instructions were to loose the animals and bring them to Him. Should they be challenged as to what they were doing, their reply was to be, 'The Lord hath need of them' (Matt. 21:3). The challenge for us as believers today is, are we prepared to make all that the Lord has entrusted to us as stewards readily available to Him?

His entry into the city on a donkey was a fulfilment of Zechariah 9:9, as quoted in Matthew 21:5: 'Tell ye the daughter of Sion, Behold, thy King cometh unto thee, meek, and sitting upon an ass, and a colt the foal of an ass.'

Mark adds additional information: 'whereon never man sat' (11:2). The colt was an unbroken, untrained animal, yet it showed no resistance as the Lord sat upon it. It recognized and gladly submitted to the Creator. There are many references in the Gospels of how the animate and the inanimate creation demonstrated a recognition of, and a response to their Creator. He was in the wilderness for forty days with the wild beasts, yet He was unharmed (Mark 1:13). They were subject to their Creator. The disciples confessed, 'Even the wind and the sea obey him' (4:41).

In the Old Testament, Jeremiah refers to how the birds are subject to God's guidance, while His people were not: 'Yea, the stork in the heaven knoweth her appointed times; and the turtle and the crane and the swallow observe the time of their coming; but my people know not the judgment of the Lord' (8:7). Isaiah speaks in a similar way of how the animals recognized their masters, while His people rebelled against Him: 'The ox knoweth his owner, and the ass his master's crib: but Israel doeth not know, my people doth not consider' (1:3).

Creation has been affected by man's fall and rebellion against God: 'For the creature was made subject to vanity, not willingly . . .' (Rom. 8:20).

The Lord Jesus did not choose to arrive in the city in a stately chariot or astride a white horse, demonstrating His power and glory; but, rather, seated upon a donkey's colt. Here was the One who could say, 'I am meek and lowly in heart' (Matt. 11:29).

Try to visualize the scene—a large company of people on their way to Jerusalem. The Lord Jesus was among them, sitting on the colt: many were going before Him, and a great multitude following after (Matt. 21:9). The roadway was strewn with the clothes that many had laid down and palm branches which they had cut from the trees. The people were shouting and singing. Their song is taken from Psalm 118:26, 'Blessed is he that cometh in the name of the Lord.' They prefaced the statement with 'Hosanna to the Son of David,' and concluded by saying 'Hosanna in the highest'; Hosanna expressing an appeal to the Lord as Saviour and Deliverer. By owning the Lord Jesus as the Son of David, they were asserting His right to reign in Jerusalem, 'the city of the great King' (Ps. 48:2). By owning Him to be the Son of the Highest, whether they understood it or not, it was paramount to acknowledging His Deity.

When the company arrived in Jerusalem and came to the temple, the Lord overthrew the tables of the moneychangers, and said, 'It is written, My house shall be called the house of prayer; but ye have made it a den of thieves.' We read here of Him healing the blind and lame. The chief priests and scribes were displeased when they saw the wonderful things that He did, and also the children continuing to cry in the temple 'Hosanna to the son of David.' In their displeasure, they said to the Lord, 'Hearest thou what these say?'. 'And Jesus saith unto them, Yea; have you never read, Out of the mouths of babes and sucklings thou hast perfected praise?' (Matt. 21:13-16; Ps. 8:2).

How fickle was the crowd who cried 'Hosanna.' Many of those who joined in that cry would soon shout with the motley throng outside Pilate's judgment hall, 'Crucify him' (Luke 23:21). Many were not genuine, and later were so easily swayed. When the choice was offered to them by Pilate to release one, Barabbas or Christ, Matthew records, 'But the chief priests and elders persuaded the multitude that they should ask Barabbas, and destroy Jesus' (27:20).

The cry of the crowd, 'Blessed is he that cometh in the name of the Lord', which proved to be insincere on their part, foreshadows a day at the end of the tribulation period when this cry will be the heartfelt language of repentant Israel. 'Ye shall not see me henceforth, till ye shall say, Blessed is he that cometh in the name of the Lord' (23:39).

5. Sitting beside the treasury: observing

'And Jesus sat over against the treasury, and beheld how the people cast money into the treasury: and many that were rich cast in much. And there came a certain poor widow, and she threw in two mites, which make a farthing. And he called unto him his disciples, and saith unto them, Verily I say unto you, That this poor widow hath cast more in, than all they which have cast into the treasury: For all they did cast in of their abundance; but she of her want did cast in all that she had, even all her living' (Mark 12: 41-44).

On this occasion the Lord Jesus is sitting in the temple beside the treasury, observing how the people cast money in. The passage says, 'many that were rich cast in much.' The Lord watched as a poor widow came in. He knew her situation: she had lost her husband. He knew her poverty: He spoke of 'her want' (v. 44). In spite of her limited resources, she threw in two mites, which make a farthing.

The Lord called His disciples to teach them, and us, a lesson in giving from this woman. He used that wonderful word, which he often used to emphasize the truth of the statement that would follow: '*Verily* I say unto you, that this poor widow hath cast more in, than all they which cast into the treasury.' He said that the rich gave much, but she gave more. He was not only saying that, in His estimation, she gave more that any one of them; she gave more than all of them together. In fact, she gave 'all that she had, even all her living' (v. 44).

What lessons can we learn from this incident?

The Lord knows every detail in connection with our giving. Notice the verb that is used: 'He *beheld*' (v. 41). He not only knows what we give, but the spirit in which we give it, 'for God loveth a cheerful giver' (2 Cor. 9:7). If the Lord was sitting beside the collection box today, would the amount of our giving or the spirit in which we give be unchanged?

In Luke's account of this incident, he says that they 'cast in unto the offerings of God' (21:4). What a thought—giving to God! May we be exercised about the grace of giving: '. . . see that ye abound in this grace also' (2 Cor. 8:7).

A church minister stood beside the collection box which was placed near the entrance door. A man rushed in a little late, and as he entered he threw a single coin into the box. As he did so, he said rather sarcastically, 'The widow's mite.' The minister said, 'Actually, it was two mites.' Rather embarrassed, the man put his hand into his pocket, took out another coin and threw it in. The minister spoke again, 'Actually, she gave all that she had!'

Giving in the shadow of the altar

When money was needed to repair the house of the Lord, 'Jehoiada the priest took a chest, and bored a hole in the lid of it, and set it beside the altar, on the right side as one cometh into the house of the Lord: and the priests that kept the door put therein all the money that was brought into the house of the Lord' (2 Kings 12:9).

As we stand beside the altar, beneath the shadow of Calvary, can we say in sincerity with Isaac Watts, 'Love so amazing, so divine, demands my heart, my life, my all'?

Giving that the Lord will not accept

'Therefore if thou bring thy gift to the altar, and there rememberest that thy brother hath ought against thee; Leave there thy gift before the altar, and go thy way; first be reconciled to thy brother, and then come and offer thy gift' (Matt. 5: 23-24).

Giving that will not be rewarded

The Lord Jesus said: 'Take heed that ye do not your alms before men, to be seen of them: otherwise ye have no reward of your Father which is in heaven . . . But when thou doest alms, let not thy left hand know what thy right hand doeth: That thine alms may be in secret: and thy Father which seeth in secret himself shall reward thee openly' (Matt. 6:1-4).

The principle of giving

The biblical principle in connection with giving is clearly stated in both the Old and New Testaments:

'Honour the Lord with thy substance, and with the firstfruits of all thine increase: So shall thy barns be filled with plenty, and thy presses shall burst out with new wine' (Proverbs 3:9).

'But this I say, He which soweth sparingly shall reap also sparingly; and he which soweth bountifully shall reap also bountifully' (2 Cor. 9:6).

6. Sitting in the upper room: instituting the Lord's Supper

The place where the Lord Jesus instituted the remembrance supper was chosen by the Lord Himself. The instructions which He gave to Peter and John were clear: 'Behold, when ye are entered into the city, there shall a man meet you, bearing a pitcher of water; follow him into the house where he entereth in. And ye shall say unto the goodman of the house, The Master saith unto thee, Where is the guestchamber, where I shall eat the Passover with my disciples? And he shall shew you a large upper room furnished: there make ready . . . and they made ready the Passover' (Luke 22:10-13).

Setting aside for the moment the Passover feast, which preceded the institution of the Lord's Supper, the room which the Lord selected for that occasion was also significant.

It was a place of refreshing

Peter and John were guided to it by following a man carrying a pitcher of water. There is no doubt that every detail of information given here is of deep significance. The man who carried the pitcher of water may represent the brethren in the assembly who refresh the hearts of the saints as they lead in worship or ministry of the word. Paul tells Philemon '. . . the bowels of the saints are refreshed by thee, brother' (v. 7), and he asks that Philemon will refresh his bowels in the Lord (v. 20). Concerning Onesimus, Paul writes, 'for he oft refreshed me' (2 Tim. 1:16). How necessary it is for the ministry of refreshment to be exercised in the assembly. Yet the most important part of all the worship of the saints as they gather to remember the Lord should be that it would refresh the heart of Christ.

It was a guestchamber

The word for guestchamber in Luke 22:11 is the same word translated as 'inn' in Luke 2:7. We remember that when the Lord Jesus was born there was no 'guestchamber'—no room for Him at His birth. How amazing that He has made a guest chamber available for all of His people, a place that we are welcome through grace as guests invited by the Lord. We hear Him say to us, as He did to the disciples on the shore of Galilee after His resurrection, 'Come and dine' (John 21:12). In his hymn, 'Sweet feast of love divine,' Edward Denny wrote:

> Here every welcome guest
> Waits, Lord, from Thee to learn
> The secrets of Thy Father's breast,
> And all Thy grace discern.

It was a large place

There was plenty of room for the thirteen who would gather on that night. The Lord had also in view the greater number who would gather after His resurrection: 'the number of names together were about one hundred and twenty' (Acts 1:15). His prayer was not only for His disciples, 'but for them also which shall believe on me through their word' (John 17:20). We can say, like the Psalmist, 'He brought me forth also into a large place' (Ps. 18:19).

It was an upper room

They would come apart from the world to be alone with Him, as Alexander Stewart expressed in his hymn, 'Lord Jesus Christ, we seek Thy face':

> *Shut in with Thee far, far above*
> *The restless world that wars below;*
> *We seek to learn and prove Thy love,*
> *Thy wisdom and Thy grace to know.*

Wherever the assembly meets for the Breaking of Bread, as holy priests we have the unspeakable privilege of entering into the immediate presence of God, within the holiest of all.

It was furnished

The only piece of furniture mentioned is a table. 'But, behold, the hand of him that betrayeth me is with me on the table' (Luke 22:21). Each of the disciples was honoured, as was Lazarus (John 12), to be one of those who sat at the table with Him; like Mephibosheth of old, who was brought by David to the king's table (2 Sam. 9:13).

Preparation was necessary

The Lord gave Peter and John instructions that the room must be prepared where the Passover would be observed, and where afterwards the Lord's Supper would be instituted. 'Go and prepare' (Luke 22:8); 'there make ready' (v. 12). Before coming to the Breaking of Bread on Lord's day mornings, may we be mindful of these words of the Lord Jesus: 'go and prepare' and 'make ready.' There is a preparation that continues throughout the week. As we read the Scriptures and meditate on what they bring before us concerning Christ, our hearts should be overflowing and we should have something of Christ to present to the Father, either silently or audibly. The Psalmist expressed his readiness to praise the Lord: 'My heart is inditing a good matter: I speak of the things which I have made touching the king; my tongue is the pen of a ready writer. Thou art fairer than the children of men . . .' (Ps. 45:1-2).

There is another aspect of preparation taught in 1 Corinthians 11:28: 'But let a man examine himself, and so let him eat of that bread, and drink of that cup.' The greater our appreciation of Christ, the more readily we will be aware of our own failings and this will lead to confession and forgiveness. 'If we confess our sins, he is faithful and just to forgive us our sins, and to cleanse us from all unrighteousness' (1 John 1:9). This preparation should not result in us staying away. The teaching is clear, 'and so let him eat of that bread, and drink of that cup.'

Well might we ponder the Master's words, 'go and prepare' and 'make ready.'

It was a place of thankfulness

The Lord gave thanks for both the bread and the cup (Luke 22:19-20). It is small wonder that with grateful hearts we can give thanks both for the bread and the cup. The brother who takes the responsibility to give thanks, does so on behalf of the whole assembly. Each believer present should be glad to say a hearty *Amen.*

We are thankful for what the emblems represent. Think of the bread: as we take it we remember the words of the Lord Jesus, 'This is my body which is given for you: this do in remembrance of me' (v.19). The believer can say, 'He took my place; His holy body was given for me.' Similarly, we gladly partake of the cup, remembering the words of our Lord: 'This cup is the new testament in my blood, which is shed for you' (v. 20). However, we should remember that it was an altogether different matter for the Lord to give thanks for the emblems. What now means life, salvation, forgiveness and joy for us, meant for Him the immeasurable sorrows of Calvary. Yet, knowing all that lay before him, still He gave thanks.

It was a place of praise

Just before leaving the upper room on that sorrowful night of the Lord's betrayal, it is moving to observe that they concluded by singing a hymn. 'And when they had sung a hymn, they went out into the Mount of Olives' (Mark 14:26). We are not told which psalm was chosen by the Lord from Israel's song book on that occasion. This is the only time in the Gospels where we read of the Lord and His disciples singing together.

CHAPTER 4

Standing

1. Standing to read: at Nazareth

'And he came to Nazareth, where he had been brought up: and, as his custom was, he went into the synagogue on the Sabbath day, and stood up for to read. And there was delivered unto him the book of the prophet Esaias. And when he had opened the book, he found the place where it was written, The Spirit of the Lord is upon me, because he hath anointed me to preach the gospel to the poor; he hath sent me to heal the brokenhearted, to preach deliverance to the captives, and recovering of sight to the blind, to set at liberty them that are bruised, To preach the acceptable year of the Lord. And he closed the book, and he gave it again to the minister, and sat down. And the eyes of all them that were in the synagogue were fastened on him. And he began to say unto them, This day is this scripture fulfilled in your ears. And all bare him witness, and wondered at the gracious words which proceeded out of his mouth. And they said, Is not this Joseph's son?' (Luke 4:16-22; Isa. 61:1-2).

It is most interesting to notice the places where the Lord is to be found in this chapter. He returns from Jordan and was led by the Spirit into the wilderness (v. 1); He is taken by the devil into a high mountain (v. 5); and to Jerusalem (v. 9); He returns to Galilee (v.14); He came to Nazareth (v.16); and He came down to Capernaum (v. 31).

The fact that the Lord Jesus was brought up in Nazareth was the fulfilment of a prophecy quoted by Matthew, 'And [Joseph] came and dwelt in a city called Nazareth: that it might be fulfilled which was spoken by the prophets, he shall be called a Nazarene' (2:23). Nowhere in the Old Testament can such a prophecy be found. Matthew refers to 'prophets' (plural), which may indicate that it was a known spoken prophecy. In a similar way Paul quotes, '. . . remember the words of the Lord Jesus, how he said, It is more blessed to give than to receive' (Acts 20:35): words that are not found in the Gospels.

This account of the Lord reading publicly from the Scriptures in the synagogue in Nazareth was not the beginning of His public ministry. Luke refers to Him returning in the power of the Spirit into Galilee, 'And he taught in their synagogues, being glorified of all' (4:14-15). However, the portion of Scripture which the Lord Jesus read at Nazareth is most significant in relation to the purpose of His ministry. Note the description of those whom He had come to bless: the poor, the brokenhearted, the captives, the blind, and the bruised.

He stood up to read, leaving an example for us to handle the Scriptures with reverence. 'He found the place where it was written'—at that time no chapters or verses were marked. He was handed the prophecy of Isaiah and His familiarity with it meant that He easily found the place in what is now 61:1-2.

He commenced reading: 'The Spirit of the Lord is upon me,'

identifying Himself as the servant of Jehovah of whom we read, 'Behold my Servant. . . I have put my Spirit upon him' (42:1). He concluded reading after the first half of a sentence, 'To preach the acceptable year of the Lord.' The remainder of the sentence which He omitted, 'and the day of vengeance of our God,' refers to a time that is still future.

When He had finished reading the Lord Jesus sat down, 'and the eyes of all them that were in the synagogue were fastened on him.' He said, 'This day is this scripture fulfilled in your ears' (v. 21). It was a very definite claim that He was the Messiah and the favourable year of the Lord had begun. At that point we read, 'And all bare him witness, and wondered at the gracious words which proceeded out of his mouth' (v. 22). Let us not miss the wonder of that moment: the *Living Word* was holding in His hand the *Written Word*, and when He spoke those present were listening to the *Spoken Word* of God.

However, the mood in the synagogue was soon to change as a result of what He proceeded to teach. 'And all they in the synagogue, when they heard these things, were filled with wrath, And rose up, and thrust him out of the city, and led him unto the brow of the hill . . . that they might cast him down headlong. But he passing through the midst of them went his way' (vv. 28-30).

2. *Standing to preach: at the Feast in Jerusalem*

'In the last day, that great day of the feast, Jesus stood and cried, saying, If any man thirst, let him come unto me, and drink. He that believeth on me, as the scripture hath said, out of his belly shall flow rivers of living water. (But this spake he of the Spirit, which they that believe on him should receive: for the Holy Ghost was not yet given; because that Jesus was not yet glorified)' (John 7:37-39).

The feast mentioned in these verses was the feast of tabernacles (v. 2), and the Lord went up to Jerusalem when the feast was at the midway point (v. 14). This feast was the last one of the year, celebrated when all of the harvest was gathered in. It commenced on a Sabbath and concluded the following Sabbath (Lev. 23:39). In Jewish reckoning, this was a seven-day period. The first day and the eighth day were of special significance: no physical work was to be done. Both days are described as 'an holy convocation.' Burnt offerings, meat offerings, and drink offerings were offered on those days.

For a period of seven days the Israelites were commanded to leave their homes and live in booths. These were constructed from palm branches, boughs of thick trees, and willows from the brook (v. 40). In the days of Nehemiah, when this long forgotten feast was restored, the booths were built on the flat roofs of their houses (Neh. 8:16).

Why did the Lord command His people to observe this feast?

What was the point of it all? 'That your generations may know that I made the children of Israel to dwell in booths, when I brought them out of the land of Egypt: I am the Lord your God' (Lev.23:43). The Lord's desire was that the people who were delivered from Egypt should remember, and the rising generation would learn about the redemption from Egypt and how the Lord had preserved His people in the wilderness.

What then is the significance of our Lord standing on the last day of the feast to make such an amazing proclamation? We have already noticed that the feast of tabernacles is spoken of as a holy convocation (a calling together, an assembly). On this occasion, the Lord Jesus issues an appeal, a call, which was directed to all present. His call was not only applicable to those who were present at the feast but to the whole world of mankind: 'If any man thirst, let him come unto me, and drink' (v. 37).

This is one of only a small number of occasions when we read of the Lord Jesus raising His voice. 'Jesus stood and cried, saying . . .' (v. 37). He stood so that all might see Him, and He cried so that all might hear Him. On another occasion when the Lord cried with a loud voice, it was to assert His deity. 'Then cried Jesus in the temple as he taught, saying, Ye both know me, and ye know whence I am: and I am not come of myself, but he that sent me is true, whom ye know not. But I know him: for I am from him, and he hath sent me' (vv. 28-20).

John records that at the grave of Lazarus, 'He cried with a loud voice, Lazarus, come forth' (11:43). Matthew in his Gospel speaks twice of the Lord crying with a loud voice on the cross (27:46, 50).

His cry at this feast in Jerusalem is reminiscent of the cry of the perfect servant in Isaiah: 'Listen, O isles, unto me; and hearken, ye people, from far' (49:1), and 'Ho, every one that thirsteth, come ye to the waters' (55:1).

The only condition required in John 7:37 is to be thirsty, to have a sense of need, as expressed in the gospel hymn, 'All the fitness He requireth is to feel your need of Him.'[1] Of all who are alive on earth today, and all who have lived in generations past, He alone could say to those with spiritual thirst, 'Let him come unto me, and drink.' He alone is able to save and to satisfy.

---

[1] 'Come, ye sinners, poor and wretched,' Joseph Hart (1712-1768).

Then He said, 'He that believeth on me', showing that the way to have our thirst quenched is by believing on Him. The Lord continued, 'as the scripture hath said.' His spoken word was always in perfect harmony with the written word.

He then spoke of the inner joy of the believer, 'out of his belly shall flow rivers of living water.' He had spoken to the Samaritan women in chapter 4 about living water, 'But whosoever drinketh of the water that I shall give him shall never thirst; but the water that I shall give him shall be in him a well of water springing up into everlasting life' (v. 14). The source of this inner joy is the indwelling Holy Spirit: '(But this spake he of the Spirit, which they that believe on Him should receive: for the Holy Ghost was not yet given; because that Jesus was not yet glorified)' (7:39).

When the command to hold the feast of tabernacles was first given, it is interesting to note the reference to water. Their booths were to be made using 'willows of the brook' (Lev. 23:40), and when the feast was revived in the days of Nehemiah, some of the booths were erected in the street of the water gate (Neh. 8:16). The Lord said that it should be a joyous occasion, 'Ye shall rejoice before the Lord your God seven days' (Lev. 23:40); 'And there was very great gladness' (Neh. 8:17).

The feast of tabernacles was a time of sacrifice: 'a burnt offering, and a meat offering, a sacrifice, and drink offerings' (Lev. 23:37). The One who stood up and cried out on the last day of the feast at Jerusalem, extending that universal invitation, did so because soon at Calvary He would offer himself as a once for all sacrifice for our sins. The sacrifices which would have been offered on that Sabbath day spoke eloquently of His sacrifice on the cross. Notice in John 7 the references to the plot of his enemies to kill him: 'the Jews sought to kill him' (v. 1); 'Why go ye about to kill me?' (v. 19).

The celebration was to remind the Israelites of their redemption from Egypt. The feast must only take place when the harvesting work was finished. Standing in Jerusalem that day was the Redeemer Himself, and one day soon He would cry in triumph on the cross, 'It is finished' (John 19:30).

3. *Standing to call Bartimaeus: outside Jericho*

The Lord Jesus was on His final journey to Jerusalem.

'And they were in the way going up to Jerusalem; and Jesus went before them: and they were amazed; and as they followed, they were afraid. And he took again the twelve, and began to tell them what things should happen unto him, Saying, Behold, we go up to Jerusalem; and the Son of man shall be delivered unto the chief priests, and unto the scribes; and they shall condemn him to death, and shall deliver him to the Gentiles: And they shall mock him, and shall scourge him, and shall spit upon him, and shall kill him: and the third day he shall rise again' (Mark 10:32-34).

How amazing that, although He knew all that He would suffer, every pain He would bear, and the ignominious death of the cross which lay before Him, we read, 'He stedfastly set his face to go to Jerusalem' (Luke 9:51). Later in the garden of Gethsemane, 'Jesus, therefore, knowing all things that should come upon him, went forth' (John 18:4). He was the perfect servant of Jehovah: '. . . therefore have I set my face like a flint, and I know that I shall not be ashamed' (Isaiah 50:7).

On the journey to Jerusalem, with still about 25 kilometres to travel, they came to Jericho and passed through it. This was the city which had been completely destroyed when the children of Israel marched around it for seven days. When the trumpets were blown by the priests, the walls fell down by the mighty power of God (Jos. 6:20). Not only was the city destroyed, but God pronounced a curse upon anyone who would attempt to rebuild it: 'Cursed be the man before the Lord, that riseth up and buildeth this city Jericho' (v. 26).

Jericho was the city of the curse; yet for 'blind Bartimaeus' there was blessing and healing the day he met with Christ not far from its gates. His disability had become linked with his name. He was known as blind Bartimaeus, and twice in the passage he is referred to as 'the blind man.' When he was asked by the Lord, 'What wilt thou that I should do unto thee?' he replied, 'Lord, that I might receive my sight' (Mark 10:51). There was no doubt in the minds of those who knew him, nor indeed in his own mind, what he needed most.

Sadly, many people in our world today don't realize that they have a spiritual need before God. They may be blessed with all five senses, yet spiritually blind to the things that matter most. 'In whom the god of this world [Satan] hath blinded the minds of them which believe not, lest the light of the glorious gospel of Christ, who is the image of God, should shine unto them' (2 Cor. 4:4).

Bartimaeus had become destitute: 'He sat by the highway side begging' (v. 46). His blindness meant that he could not enjoy many of the simple pleasures of life. He could not marvel at the beauty of the sunset, nor look heavenward to wonder at the stars. He could not appreciate the beauty of the flowers and trees; he could not admire the mountains and hills, nor look into the faces of family and friends.

One sat alone beside the highway begging;
His eyes were blind, the light he could not see.
He clutched his rags and shivered in the shadows,
Then Jesus came and bade his darkness flee.

Oswald Jeffrey Smith

The day began like any other. A friend guided Bartimaeus to his usual place beside the highway and he settled down in the hope that at least a few charitable people would take pity on him a drop a few coins into his lap. After some time, he heard a crowd approaching and he realized that something unusual was happening, so he called out and *asked what it meant* (Luke 18:36). What is the answer to the question asked by Bartimaeus? What did the noise and the commotion and the crowd mean? The answer came, 'Jesus of Nazareth passeth by.'

On the road that day was the Son of God incarnate, who had come down from the glory of Heaven to this world of sin. He was now on His last journey to Jerusalem, where He would suffer outside the city wall and die for a world of lost sinners, and for the poor mortal who sat beside the highway begging.

Oh teach me what it meaneth:
That cross uplifted high,
With One, the Man of Sorrows,
Condemned to bleed and die.
Oh teach me what it cost Thee
To make a sinner whole;
And teach me, Saviour, teach me
The value of a soul.

Lucy Ann Bennett

Perhaps he had heard of Jesus from those who passed by on the highway. He had heard their accounts of how He had healed many people of their ailments, and also how the blind were made to see. Bartimaeus could not see, but he could hear. How often the Scriptures promise blessing to those who hear and respond to the word of God. 'Incline your ear, and come unto me: hear, and your soul shall live' (Isaiah 55:3). The Lord Jesus said, 'He that heareth my word, and believeth on him that sent me, hath everlasting life' (John 5:24). Bartimaeus realized the urgency of the situation; within earshot was the only person in the world who could meet his need and give him his sight. What he didn't realize was that the Lord was passing on the highway for the last time, and it was his final opportunity.

He began to cry out and say, 'Jesus, thou son of David, have mercy on me.' Not only had he heard of what Jesus could do, but something of who He was, the son of David, the Messiah. He cried out repeatedly, in spite of the many people who told him to be quiet. In fact, the more they tried to silence him, the more determined and more vocal he became. He was persistent and the Lord was not about to ignore his call. 'And ye shall seek me, and find me, when ye shall search for me with all your heart' (Jer. 29:13).

Then we read that amazing statement, '*And Jesus stood still, and commanded him to be called*' (10:49). The Lord Jesus was on the most momentous journey ever undertaken in the history of the world. Such eternal and weighty matters were to be dealt with fully and finally at Calvary. Yet for one man, Bartimaeus, a poor blind beggar, the Son of God stopped on the highway and commanded His disciples to call him.

Do we not see here an example of how the call of the gospel

is to be sounded out? The Lord gave the command to His servants, 'Go ye into all the world, and preach the gospel to every creature,' and they issue the gospel call in His name (Mark 16:15). Twice in Scripture the Lord Jesus is given the lovely title, 'the Saviour of the world' (John 4:42; 1 John 4:14). What a glorious truth it is—there is a Saviour available to every person alive on planet earth today. At the same time, He is the Saviour of the individual, as illustrated in the blessing that Bartimaeus experienced. The disciples said, 'Be of good comfort, rise; he calleth thee' (Mark 10:49). What a message, what a balm to the troubled heart of this poor man. 'Jesus of Nazareth is interested in you; He has heard your cry and He has stopped. He is calling you.'

'Casting away his garment, Bartimaeus rose' (v. 50). He threw away his outer garment. He didn't want anything to hinder him or hold him back as he came to Jesus. Those who would seek the Lord often have to discard anything that would hinder them. The question which the Lord asked him was, 'What wilt thou that I should do unto thee?' He replied, 'Lord, that I might receive my sight.' Bartimaeus had called out to Jesus of Nazareth, the son of David, but now he acknowledges Him as Lord. 'For whosoever shall call upon the name of the Lord shall be saved' (Rom. 10:13).

The Lord had asked him, 'What wilt thou?'. Salvation is the surrender of the will to Christ. Right at the end of the Bible, on its last page, the message is still 'whosoever will, let him take the water of life freely' (Rev. 22:17).

What did the encounter with Christ mean to this man? The Lord said (1) 'Go thy way'; (2) 'Thy faith hath made thee whole.' Immediately, he received his sight and followed Jesus in the way. We notice the instantaneous blessing he received. The Lord Himself described what happened to Bartimaeus as he was made whole. There was no referral to anyone else, no treatment needed, no recovery period. These words aptly describe the experience of a person today who repents of their sins and believes on the Lord Jesus Christ as their Saviour. They are 'made whole', made complete: 'Ye are complete in him' (Col. 2:10). As you read these lines, maybe you are still searching. Only in Christ can you know what it is to be 'made whole.'

As Joshua and his armies battled against the five kings of the Amorites, the sun stood still (Jos. 10:13). That was a wonderful miracle; yet something infinitely more wonderful took place when the Son of God stood still on earth, called a poor blind man, and healed him.

The record of this healing miracle is also recorded in Luke 18 and Matthew 20. They give a few more details about the incident. Matthew tells us that it was compassion which caused Christ to stop and heal the man. He also adds that Jesus touched his eyes. Luke adds that, when Bartimaeus followed Jesus, he did so glorifying God. He also mentions that the crowd who witnessed the miracle 'gave praise unto God.'

At the beginning of His public ministry the Lord Jesus read from Isaiah 61 in the synagogue at Nazareth: 'The Spirit of the Lord is upon me, because he hath anointed me to preach the gospel to the poor . . . recovering of sight to the blind' (Luke 4:18). The first spoken words in creation were, 'Let there be light' (Gen. 1:3). How can a person, who has been long blinded by the devil, be brought into the light and liberty of God's salvation? 'For God, who commanded the light to shine out of darkness, hath shined in our hearts, to give the light of the knowledge of the glory of God in the face of Jesus Christ' (2 Cor. 4:6).

4. Standing to witness [the] good confession: before the Governor

How significant are these words! Pilate was the Roman governor, but only of a limited territory, Judea, and only for a limited time of about 10 years, A.D. 27-37. Standing before him was the Lord Jesus, the One of whom the prophet Isaiah said 'the government shall be upon his shoulder . . . of the increase of his government and peace there shall be no end' (9:6-7).

Matthew quotes from the prophet Micah, 'And thou Bethlehem . . . out of thee shall come a Governor, that shall rule my people Israel' (2:6). He was the true Governor who will ultimately govern over unlimited territory, 'He shall have dominion also from sea to sea, and from the river unto the ends of the earth' (Ps. 72:8). His government shall know no end. 'And the Lord God shall give unto him the throne of his father David: And he shall reign over the house of Jacob for ever; and of his kingdom there shall be no end' (Luke 1:32-33).

The Lord Jesus foretold that He would be handed over by the chief priests and scribes to the Gentiles. 'Behold, we go up to Jerusalem; and the Son of man shall be betrayed unto the chief priests and unto the scribes, and they shall condemn him to death, And shall deliver him to the Gentiles to mock, and to scourge, and to crucify him; and the third day he shall rise again' (Matt. 20:18-19).

The record of how the Jews delivered Christ to Pilate is found in John 18:28: 'Then led they Jesus from Caiaphas unto the hall of judgment: and it was early; and they themselves went not into the judgment hall, lest they should be defiled; but that they might eat the Passover.' What utter hypocrites they were. Being a Gentile environment, they would not go into the judgment hall in case there was any leaven and they would be defiled; yet they were guilty of the most heinous of crimes by rejecting Christ, and they carried the ultimate responsibility for His crucifixion. The Lord described them as, 'Ye blind guides, which strain at a gnat, and swallow a camel' (Matt. 23:24).

It was for this reason that in John's account we read of Pilate going out and coming into the judgment hall to speak to the Jews. Going out, 18:29, 38; 19:4, 13; coming in: 18:33; 19:1, 9. When Pilate asked the Jews the question, 'What accusation bring ye against this man?', they said, 'If he were not a malefactor, we would not have delivered him up unto thee' (18:29-30). Their answer must have been totally unconvincing to Pilate.

There were three accusations brought against the Lord Jesus as He stood before Pilate. They are all found in Luke 23:2. 'And the whole multitude . . . began to accuse him, saying, We found this fellow perverting the nation, and forbidding to give tribute to Caesar, saying that he himself is Christ a King.'

Charge 1. *Perverting the nation.* This accusation was invalid; never did the Lord Jesus recommend rebellion against the nation. He taught 'Blessed are the peacemakers' (Matt. 5:9). How remarkable it is that, when faced later with a choice between Barabbas, who had already been tried and found guilty of sedition, and Christ, they said 'Not this man, but Barabbas' (John 18:40).

Charge 2. *Forbidding to give tribute to Caesar.* Again this accusation was without foundation. 'Then saith he unto them, Render therefore unto Caesar the things which are Caesar's; and unto God the things that are God's' (Matt 22:21).

Charge 3. *Saying that He Himself is Christ a King*. He did claim to be Christ and He was born a king. When Peter confessed Him at Caesarea Philippi, saying, 'Thou art the Christ, the Son of the living God,' the Lord commended Peter: 'flesh and blood hath not revealed it unto thee, but my Father which is in heaven' (Matt. 16:16-17). In His infancy the wise men sought Him saying, 'Where is he that is born King of the Jews?' (Matt. 2:2).

Before Caiphas, the charge against Him was that He claimed to be the Christ, the Son of God (see Matt. 26:63). Such a claim was blasphemy in their eyes. Before Pilate the charge was that He had falsely claimed to be the King of Israel (see Luke 23:2-3), and therefore guilty of insurrection.

How wonderful that, in a coming day, Israel will confess, as Nathanael did, 'Thou art the Son of God; thou art the King of Israel' (John 1:49). 'Thou art the Son of God,'— You never were guilty of blasphemy; 'Thou art the King of Israel,'— You never were guilty of insurrection. This will be Israel's confession when the King returns to earth at the end of the tribulation period.

Pilate gave his verdict; he repeated three times, 'I find no fault in this man' (Luke 23:4, 14, 22). Finally, he washed his hands before the multitude saying, 'I am innocent of the blood of this just person: see ye to it' (Matt. 27:24).

It is noteworthy that among those involved in the arrest, trial and crucifixion of Christ, there were at least six individuals who attested to his innocence.

Pilate the judge: four times he affirmed his innocence (John 18:38; 19:4, 6; Matt. 27:24).

Pilate's wife: 'His wife sent unto him saying, Have thou nothing to do with that just man' (Matt. 27:19).

Judas: 'I have betrayed the innocent blood' (Matt. 27:4).

Herod: 'No, nor yet Herod: for I sent to him; and, lo, nothing worthy of death is done unto him' (Luke 23:15).

The Centurion: 'Certainly this was a righteous man' (Luke 23:47).

The malefactor: 'This man hath done nothing amiss' (Luke 23:41).

All four Gospels speak of the Lord's silence when he stood before Pilate. He had nothing to say in His own defence. 'But Jesus yet answered nothing; so that Pilate marvelled' (Mark 15:5). The prophecy in Isaiah was fulfilled, 'He was oppressed, and he was afflicted, yet he opened not his mouth: he is brought as a lamb to the slaughter, and as a sheep before her shearers is dumb, so he openeth not his mouth' (53:7). Note the repetition of the statement, 'he openeth not his mouth.'

A lamb brought to the slaughter is silent: it knows nothing of what lies before it, and that its life is soon to be ended. A sheep before her shearers is silent: it has no knowledge that what lies before it will be a painless experience. But, 'Jesus therefore, *knowing all things* that should come upon him, went forth . . .' (John 18:4).

Paul speaks of 'Christ Jesus, who before Pontius Pilate

witnessed [the] good confession' (1 Tim. 6:13). Peter says, 'Who, when he was reviled, reviled not again; when he suffered, he threatened not; but committed himself to him that judgeth righteously' (1 Peter 2:23).

Well might we say with Philip Bliss:

> *Bearing shame and scoffing rude,*
> *In my place condemned He stood;*
> *Sealed my pardon with His blood;*
> *Hallelujah! what a Saviour!*

5. Standing to speak peace to His disciples: in the upper room

'Then the same day at evening, being the first day of the week . . . came Jesus and stood in the midst, and saith unto them, Peace be unto you . . . And after eight days again his disciples were within, and Thomas with them: then came Jesus, the doors being shut, and stood in the midst, and said, Peace be unto you' (John 20: 19, 26).

The One whose body had lain within the garden tomb for three days and three nights now stands, in living power, in the midst of His own.

The risen Lord standing in the midst of His own in the upper room is a thrilling account of an event which took place on the day of His resurrection. It was the first day of the week, and He appeared to them again on the first day of the week, eight days later. These are the first and second appearances to the disciples after His resurrection. The third appearance, to seven disciples, is recorded by John, 'This is now the third time that Jesus shewed himself to his disciples, after that he was risen from the dead' (21:14).

The believer today has two responsibilities in relation to the first day of the week.

1. To gather with other believers to break bread: 'And upon the first day of the week . . . the disciples came together to break bread . . .' (Acts 20:7).

2. To set aside our offering for the Lord: 'Upon the first day of the week let every one of you lay by him in store, as God hath prospered him . . .' (1 Cor. 16:2).

When we gather in His name we have the promise of His presence with us: 'For where two or three are gathered together in my name, there am I in the midst of them' (Matt. 18:20). The Lord's promise here means that His presence is just as real today in the midst of His gathered people as it was when He was physically present in the upper room. The Lord in the midst does not mean that He is in the centre of wherever the table with the emblems may be positioned; His promise means that He is as near to one believer as another there.

What were the features in John 20 that we can enjoy as we gather in His Name today?

1. The *reality* of His presence with us (v. 19).

2. The *reminder* of how much He suffered on our account: 'He showed unto them his hands and his side' (v. 20).

3. The *rejoicing* in the fact that He is alive: 'Then were the disciples glad, when they saw the Lord' (v. 20).

4. The *relief* they experienced. They had gathered in fear with the doors locked, but the One who appeared in their midst spoke words of peace (vv.19, 21, 26). He had left them with

the words, 'These things I have spoken unto you, that in me ye might have peace' (16:33). Between chapter 16 and chapter 20 He had been to Calvary where, as Paul records, '[He] made peace through the blood of his cross' (Col. 1:20).

5. The *responsibility* to go forth in His name with the message concerning the remission of sins: '. . . as my Father hath sent me, even so send I you . . .' (vv. 21-23).

6. The *reception* of the Holy Spirit: 'Receive ye the Holy Ghost' (v. 22). The Lord was speaking prophetically of the coming of the Holy Spirit on the day of Pentecost (Acts 2:1-4).

7. The *response* of every believer should surely be to exclaim, as Thomas did long ago, 'My Lord and my God' (v. 28).

6. Standing to guide the fishermen: on the shore at Tiberias

A full list of the twelve disciples is mentioned in Matthew 10:2-4, Mark 3:16-19, and Luke 6:14-16. After the death of Judas and before the selection of Matthias (Acts 1:26), there were eleven disciples (Acts 1:13-14). In the upper room after the resurrection, with Thomas absent, there were ten (John 20:24). Seven of the twelve go fishing together Peter, Thomas, Nathanael, James, John, and two other disciples (John 21:2). Three, Peter, James and John, were with the Lord on the Mount of Transfiguration (Luke 9:28), in the house of Jairus when his daughter was raised from the dead (8:51), and in the Garden of Gethsemane when He prayed (Matt. 26:37). Two were sent to prepare the upper room, Peter and John (Luke 22:8); but there was one disciple at the cross—John (John 19:26).

Peter said 'I go a fishing' (John 21:3). As on many other

occasions, he took the lead. His name is given first here and he is mentioned first in every list of the disciples in Scripture. This surely was regress, not progress. On the day the Lord called him on the shore of Lake Gennesaret, He said, 'Fear not, from henceforth thou shalt catch men. And when they had brought their ships to land, they forsook all and followed him' (Luke 5:10-11)

The other six disciples said, 'We also go with thee.' We are reminded of the influence we have on those around us for good or ill. They entered into a ship immediately, perhaps indicating impetuosity, and that night they caught nothing. In our lives, are there not times of barrenness, when there is very little, if anything, for God? Maybe for the moment they had forgotten what the Lord had taught them as they left the upper room with regard to bearing fruit, 'Without me ye can do nothing' (John 15:5). The same lesson applies to fishing; without Him no fruit, and without Him no fish.

'But when the morning was now come, Jesus stood on the shore: but the disciples knew not that it was Jesus' (21:4). Was it the early morning mist that obscured their vison of Him or, as with the two on the Emmaus road, were 'their eyes holden that they should not know him' (Luke 24:16)? The Lord spoke to them saying, 'Children have ye any meat? They answered him, No. And he said unto them, Cast the net on the right side of the ship, and ye shall find. They cast therefore, and now they were not able to draw it for the multitude of fishes' (John 21:5-6). The first disciple to recognize who the person was on the shore was John. He said to Peter, 'It is the Lord.' Was it in the great catch of fish that John caught a glimpse of the miraculous power of Christ?

Sometimes when we see the Lord working in our lives we too have to stand back and acknowledge, 'It is the Lord.' God's people of old had to acknowledge, 'This is the Lord's doing; it is marvellous in our eyes' (Ps. 118:23).

Hasty as ever, Peter swam the short distance of about 100 metres to the shore. The others came in the boat, 'dragging the net with fishes. As soon then as they were come to land, they saw a fire of coals there, and fish laid thereon, and bread' (John 21:8-9). It's worth noticing what the Lord said to the disciples. 'Bring of the fish which ye have *now* caught' (v. 10). Then Peter 'drew the net to land, full of great fishes, an hundred and fifty and three: and for all there were so many, yet was not the net broken' (v. 11). What a contrast between the '*then*' of a long night, when they caught nothing, and the '*now*', when He was directing their efforts with such success. How gracious the Lord was to attribute the catch of fish to them.

So it is with those who serve the Lord today. He gives them the ability, the opportunity, and the physical strength required to serve Him, and will ultimately reward their efforts for Him.

There were two catches of fish: those that the Lord already had on the fire, and the 153 in the net. There are souls won for Christ without any human instrumentality, and others that the Lord saves as a result of the witness of another believer. We see this illustrated in John 1. The Lord used John the Baptist (vv. 29, 36), Andrew (v. 41), Philip (v. 45); yet verse 43 records, 'Jesus would go forth into Galilee and findeth Philip.' The Lord alone called Philip; no one else was involved.

Why a fire of coals on the shore? Was it to remind Peter of another fire of coals at which he had stood and warmed himself in the house of Caiaphas? How meaningful are the words, 'And Peter stood with them' (John 18:18). It was in that house that Peter denied the Lord three times, as the Lord had foretold he would. Three times the Lord asked Peter, 'Simon, son of Jonas, Lovest thou me?' (John 21).

The first time, the question was, 'Lovest thou me more than these?' (v. 15). Some think that 'these' refers to the other disciples, amongst whom was John. Could Peter claim that he loved the Lord more than John? Would the Lord introduce a relative aspect to the love of believers towards Him? Surely this is something that He alone can measure? Perhaps it refers to the fish and fishing, the career that he had left behind and sacrificed for the cause of Christ.

Peter's reply was, 'Yea, Lord; thou knowest that I love thee. He saith unto him, Feed my lambs.' The Lord repeated the question, 'Simon, son of Jonas, lovest thou me?' Peter's reply was the same: 'Yea, Lord; thou knowest that I love thee. He saith unto him, Feed my sheep' (v. 16). The third time the Lord asked the same question, Peter was grieved. 'He said unto him, Lord, thou knowest all things; thou knowest that I love thee. Jesus saith unto him, Feed my sheep' (v. 17).

In verse 15 the Lord said 'Feed my lambs'; in verse 16, '[Shepherd] my sheep'; and in verse 17, 'Feed my sheep.' The lambs perhaps indicate those who have recently been saved, and need to be nurtured and fed. The sheep need to be shepherded and cared for, and they also need to be fed. The three statements together sum up the elders' responsibility (Acts 20:28). The Lord was saying to Peter, 'LOVE ME; FEED MINE.'

With reference to the Chief Shepherd, who is our Lord Jesus, Isaiah says, 'He shall feed his flock like a shepherd: he shall gather the lambs with his arm, and carry them in his bosom, and shall gently lead those that are with young' (40:11). Each of the three times that Peter affirmed his love for Christ, he used the same word *phileo*, meaning 'to be fond of', or 'to have an affection for' (James Strong). The word used by the Lord in His first and second questions to Peter was the word *agapao*, meaning 'to love with a deliberate assent of the will.' When the Lord asks the final time, 'Lovest thou me?' the word He uses is *phileo*, the same word used by Peter. Peter's love could never rise to the degree suggested in the Lord's first two questions. William Walsham How wrote:

> *It is most wonderful to know*
> *His love for me so free and sure;*
> *But 'tis more wonderful to see*
> *My love for Him so faint and poor.*

CHAPTER 5

Walking

1. *Walking by the River Jordan: beginning His ministry*

'. . . John stood, and two of his disciples; And looking upon Jesus as he walked, he saith, Behold the Lamb of God!' (John 1:35-36).

It is a delightful study to follow the footsteps of the Lord Jesus in this world. In this passage He is walking beside the river Jordan. It is significant that John the Baptist is standing; perhaps indicating that his work was at an end. The Lord Jesus is walking; the work of His public ministry had just begun. John identifies Him as the Lamb of God (v. 29). What a moment in the world's history.

Peter later wrote of the *selection* of the Lamb: '. . . as of a lamb without blemish and without spot: Who verily was foreordained before the foundation of the world, but was manifest in these last times for you' (1 Pet. 1:19-20). When He was identified (pointed out) by John the Baptist, this was His manifestation as the Lamb of God. He was the fulfilment of Abraham's prophecy to Isaac at Mount Moriah, 'My son, God will provide himself a lamb for a burnt offering' (Gen 22:8).

His *spotlessness* is spoken of by Peter in verse 19, 'the precious blood of Christ, as of a lamb without blemish and without spot.' This was the fulfilment of the stipulation of Exodus 12:5, 'Your lamb shall be without blemish.' The examination of the lamb from the tenth until the fourteenth day of the month was by external observation only, but the additional phrase used by Peter, 'and without spot', looks beyond the external and includes what was known to God alone, His inner thoughts and motives. Within and without, He was the spotless Lamb of God.

Further thoughts which are conveyed to our minds concerning the Lamb of God are, His *silence*, His *submission*, and His *sacrifice*. '. . . yet He opened not His mouth: He is brought as a lamb to the slaughter . . .' (Isa. 53:7). So John announced, 'Behold the Lamb of God, which taketh away the sin of the world.'

His *supremacy*: 'And I beheld, and, lo, in the midst of the throne . . . stood a Lamb as it had been slain' (Rev. 5:6).

> *Every knee in heaven is bending*
> *To the Lamb for sinners slain;*
> *Every voice and harp is swelling,*
> *'Worthy is the lamb to reign.'*
> James G. Deck

His *sovereignty*: 'And I looked, and, lo, a Lamb stood on the mount Sion' (Rev. 14:1).

In John 1:1, He is the Word of God, a name which is also found in Revelation 19:13. In John 1 He is the Word of God who came in grace; in Revelation 19 He is The Word of God who will come in judgment. Just as we use words to express our thoughts to others, as the Word He is the expression to us of all that God is in His person. John says, 'And the Word was made flesh, and dwelt among us, (and we beheld his glory, the glory as of the only begotten of the Father,) full of grace and truth' (1:14).

Not only did the Lord Jesus speak the word of God, 'And with many such parables spake he the word unto them' (Mark 4:33); but in Himself He was the Word who John said 'dwelt among us.'

> *True image of the Infinite,*
> *Whose essence is concealed;*
> *Brightness of uncreated light;*
> *The heart of God revealed.*
> Josiah Conder

Three times in John 1 it is declared by different individuals that He is the Son of God. By John the apostle in verse 1, 'The Word was God'; by John the Baptist in verse 34, 'And I saw, and bare record that this is the Son of God'; and by Nathanael in verse 49. He said to the Lord Jesus, 'Rabbi, thou art the Son of God; thou art the King of Israel.'

Further assertions of His deity follow in the ensuing chapters. The blind man who had received his sight was asked by the Lord, 'Dost thou believe on the Son of God?' He replied, 'Lord, I believe. And he worshipped him' (9:35, 38).

The Lord Himself asked, 'Say ye of him, whom the Father hath sanctified, and sent into the world, Thou blasphemest; because I said, I am the Son of God?' (10:36).

Martha of Bethany said, 'Yea, Lord: I believe that thou art

the Christ, the Son of God, which should come into the world' (11:27).

Thomas: 'And Thomas answered and said unto him, My Lord and my God' (20:28).

There are at least seven personal confessions to the deity of Christ in John's Gospel. How fitting that John should conclude chapter 20 with the words, 'But these are written, that ye might believe that Jesus is the Christ, the Son of God; and that believing ye might have life through his name' (v. 31).

Like Thomas, may we bow low before Him and exclaim from a contrite heart, 'My Lord and my God.'

When John the Baptist had said 'Behold the Lamb of God', two of John's disciples who heard him speak followed Jesus. One was Andrew, Simon Peter's brother. The other unnamed disciple may have been John, who very often leaves out his own name and calls himself 'the disciple whom Jesus loved.' The previous day they had heard John saying 'Behold the Lamb of God, which taketh away the sin of the world.' When once again they hear him saying 'Behold the Lamb of God!', they follow Jesus (v. 36).

Surely, the result of all our efforts to spread the gospel by whatever means is that people might be attracted to Christ and follow Him. 'For even hereunto were ye called: because Christ also suffered for us, leaving us an example, that ye should follow his steps' (1 Pet. 2:21). Here we have the footsteps of the Shepherd. In the Song of Solomon 1:8 we have the footsteps of the flock. It is His desire that the footsteps of the flock would closely follow the footsteps of the Shepherd.

> *Oh let me see Thy footmarks,*
> *And in them plant mine own;*
> *My hope to follow duly*
> *Is in Thy strength alone.*
> John Ernest Bode

2. *Walking by the Sea of Galilee: calling His disciples*

'Now as he walked by the Sea of Galilee, he saw Simon and Andrew his brother casting a net into the sea: for they were fishers. And Jesus said unto them, Come ye after me, and I will make you to become fishers of men. And straightway they forsook their nets, and followed him. And when he had gone a little farther thence, he saw James the son of Zebedee, and John his brother, who also were in the ship mending their nets. And straightway he called them: and they left their father Zebedee in the ship with the hired servants, and went after him' (Mark 1:16-20).

In these verses we have the record of how the Lord Jesus called four fishermen to be His disciples. They were Simon Peter and Andrew, James and John, two pairs of brothers. In the New Testament, when we read of the disciples, we remember that each one had a first meeting with Christ, though not all are recorded. In John 1 we find the conversions of Andrew, Simon Peter, Philip, and Nathanael.

Then there is their call to service, which in their case entailed leaving their secular occupation to forsake all and follow Him. The call of the four fishermen is outlined in Mark 1:16-20 and Luke 5:1-11. Matthew's call to service is given in Matthew 9:9: 'And as Jesus passed forth from thence, he saw a man, named Matthew, sitting at the receipt of custom: and he saith unto him, Follow me. And he arose, and followed him.'

Every believer is called to work for the Lord in some way. Like Paul on the road to Damascus, we should ask the Lord, 'What wilt thou have me to do?' For most of us, this will be working in a secular job to earn enough to support our family and be able to give to those in need: 'Let him that stole steal no more: but rather let him labour, working with his hands the thing which is good, that he may have to give to him that needeth' (Eph. 4:28). Paul himself worked at times, tent making (Acts 18:1-3). The vital matter for every Christian is to follow the will of God.

We find the call to apostleship in Luke 6:12-16. Having spent the whole night on the mountain in prayer, in the morning the Lord called His disciples and from their number 'He chose twelve, whom also he named Apostles' (v. 13). How privileged these men were to be in the company of Christ for more than two years, to learn from Him, the Prince of teachers, and to be entrusted with the task of carrying forward His work after the Lord had ascended to Heaven. What an honour He conferred upon them. In the description of the heavenly city, we read, 'And the wall of the city had twelve foundations, and in them the names of the twelve apostles of the Lamb' (Rev. 21:14).

In the understanding of the New Testament passages where they are mentioned, it is helpful to see the initial call of the disciples; that is, their conversion, their call to service, and finally their call to apostleship.

It is interesting to note the different references to fishing nets. Simon and Andrew were *casting* a net (Mark 1:16). This was their daily occupation, 'they were fishers', and they were experienced at their trade. Luke 5 says that Simon owned the boat (v. 3), so they had known a measure of success at fishing.

As He walked along the shore, the Lord said, 'Come ye after me, and I will make you to become fishers of men' (v. 17). This was an experience they had not known, and a skill they had not yet acquired. However, the Lord had promised His enabling: 'I will make you to become . . .' We may feel inadequate for the work to which the Lord has called us, but let us ever remember the promise of His enabling grace, 'I will make you to become . . .'

James and John were *mending* their nets (v. 19). With constant use, the nets had been damaged and torn, and they had lost their usefulness. There were holes where fish could pass through and be lost. What a lesson for us who seek to win souls for Christ. Maybe we too need to spend some time mending our nets. How we need to search our hearts daily under the searchlight of God's word. Is there an unconfessed sin that we need to repent of before the Lord? Is there a brother or sister that we once enjoyed happy fellowship with, but something has arisen to mar that fellowship? Before we launch out into the deep and expect God to reward our efforts, we need to spend time mending our nets, as James and John did. Only when the nets were mended were they fully effective and useful for the purpose for which they were made.

The fishermen were *washing* their nets (Luke 5:2). Debris would be caught in the nets; they would become entangled with weeds and need to be washed to maintain their efficiency. We live in a defiling world; how needful it is for us to seek daily cleansing by 'the washing of water by the word' (Eph. 5:26). The Lord Jesus prayed, 'Sanctify them through thy truth: Thy word is truth' (John 17:17).

We read of a net that was *broken* (Luke 5:6). The Lord had borrowed Peter's ship as a platform from which to speak to the multitude gathered on the shore. He asked Peter to take it out a little from the land. Anyone who has tried to preach in the open air by the seaside will know that it's better to have the sea behind you, as it helps to carry your voice forward. When the Lord had finished speaking, He asked Peter to 'launch out into the deep, and let down your nets for a draught' (v. 4). Having spent the night fishing and caught nothing, Peter said, '. . . nevertheless at thy word I will let down the net.' He spoke with a measure of scepticism and unbelief in his heart.

There was a great number of fish in the net, and the net broke. Their ship was full, and the ship owned by their partners was also full, so some fish were lost because of the broken net. The boat began to sink, and Peter realized the folly of his unbelief. 'When Simon Peter saw it, he fell down at Jesus' knees, saying, Depart from me; for I am a sinful man, O Lord' (v. 8).

It is worthy of note that, after the resurrection, when the risen Lord directed the disciples where they should fish, Peter obeyed without question, and the result was a great catch of fish brought to the shore. On that occasion the comment is added, 'and for all there were so many, yet was not the net broken' (John 21:11).

'And when they had brought their ships to land, they forsook all, and followed him' (Luke 5:11). 'All' included the ships, the nets, the servants, their father, and their business: they forsook all. What caused them to sacrifice so much? It was so that they might follow Him.

3. Walking on the Sea of Galilee: demonstrating His power

'And in the fourth watch of the night Jesus went unto them, walking on the sea' (Matt. 14:25).

After the feeding of the five thousand, the Lord stayed to send the multitude away while His disciples went ahead by ship to go to the other side of the Sea of Galilee.

When the crowd dispersed the Lord went up into a mountain alone to pray. Meanwhile the disciples in the ship were engulfed in a fierce storm. It was dark, the wind was against them, hindering their progress, and they were 'toiling in rowing' (Mark 6:48). Even though the Lord Jesus was a considerable distance away and the night was dark, Mark records that He saw them, and Matthew records that in the fourth watch of the night Jesus went unto them

If the disciples were afraid because of the storm, their fear intensified when they saw the figure of a man walking on the sea. Their initial thought was that this was a spirit. How reassuring for them to hear the voice they knew so well, saying, 'Be of good cheer: it is I; be not afraid' (v. 50). When the Lord climbed into the ship, the wind ceased. The disciples' fear was turned to amazement: 'they were sore amazed in themselves beyond measure, and wondered' (v. 51).

There were three miracles: 1. The Lord walked on the sea; 2. The Lord stilled the storm; 3. The Lord brought them immediately to their destination.

Walking on the sea — this was contrary to at least two laws of science. The law of gravity, discovered by Isaac Newton around 1687, and the law of buoyancy, propounded by Archimedes. While Newton and Archimedes laid claim to the discovery of these laws, the One who walked on the sea was the Son of God who made the laws at the beginning. He could assert His authority as Creator to control their forces according to His will.

Stilling the storm — He alone had the power to speak to the elements, and they obeyed Him. The One who caused the storm to rise in the days of Jonah was able on this occasion to cause the storm to cease. 'The Lord sent out a great wind into the sea . . . God prepared a vehement east wind' (Jonah 1:4; 4:8).

Bringing them to their destination — 'Then they willingly received him into the ship: and immediately the ship was at the land whither they went' (John 6:21). Why were the disciples so amazed at these demonstrations of the miraculous power of Christ, considering they had recently witnessed the miracle of the feeding of the five thousand? The reason is given in Mark 6:52: 'For they considered not the miracle of the loaves: for their heart was hardened.'

Matthew records how Peter walked on the water to go to Jesus, but when he saw the boisterous wind and waves he began to sink. He cried out, 'Lord, save me.' 'And immediately Jesus stretched forth his hand, and caught him, and said unto him, O thou of little faith, wherefore didst thou doubt?' (14:30-31).

What lessons can we glean from this delightful story? By our actions or in our thoughts we ought never to limit the power of our omnipotent Lord. May we not forget His blessings in the past, and may it lead us to trust Him for the future.

The boisterous sea was what troubled the disciples most, but it was under His feet and subject to His control. How reassuring that, whatever storm may sweep the sky of our lives, He knows when it is raging and is able to speak the word, 'Peace, be still.'

The Lord on the mountain, while the disciples were in the storm on the sea, is a picture for us of our great High Priest at the right hand of God. We are still travelling on the sea of life, still exposed to dangers. He sees, knows, and cares, and He draws near to succour and meet our need. When He comes to us in the darkest hour, may we hear Him say as of old, 'Be of good cheer: it is I; be not afraid.'

4. Walking in the temple: affirming His deity

'And it was at Jerusalem the feast of the dedication, and it was winter. And Jesus walked in the temple in Solomon's porch' (John 10:22-23).

The feast of the dedication is not one of the seven feasts of Jehovah outlined in Leviticus 23, and this is the only place in the New Testament where it is mentioned. It has been celebrated by the Jews since 164 B.C., as the feast of Hanukkah. In 169 B.C. the ruler of Syria, Antiochus Epiphanes, invaded Jerusalem. He was infamous in Jewish history, and referred to as 'Antiochus the wicked'. He destroyed a large part of the city and slaughtered many of its inhabitants. He went into the Temple and carried away the golden altar, the lampstand, and other sacred vessels. He desecrated the brazen altar by offering the sacrifice of a pig to the Greek god, Jupiter.

After an uprising of the Jews against him in 164 B.C., the Syrians were driven from Jerusalem. The altar was demolished, rebuilt, and consecrated amid great rejoicing. This feast of dedication (Hanukkah) became the celebration of that victory, and is observed by the Jews to the present day. It was also known as the feast of lights. A feature of its observance is the lighting of candles to remember the triumph of light over darkness. How amazing, then, that the One who was walking in the precincts of the temple while this feast was being observed had announced in the previous chapter, 'I am the light of the world' (9:5).

Solomon's porch was a roofed portico on the eastern side of Herod's temple. On that day there walked in its precincts the Son of David (Matt. 1:1), who once proclaimed, 'A greater than Solomon is here' (12:42). It is referred to in Acts 3:11. When Peter and John met the lame man at the Beautiful gate of the temple, Peter said to him, 'In the name of Jesus Christ of Nazareth rise up and walk,' and immediately he was healed. A crowd of people, when they saw the miracle, followed the two apostles into the porch. Peter preached concerning the death and resurrection of Christ, and urged the crowd to 'Repent ye therefore, and be converted, that your sins may be blotted out . . .' (v. 19).

What a response there was to Peter's message: 'Howbeit many of them which heard the word believed; and the number of the men was about five thousand' (4:4). Again we read of great healing and blessing at Solomon's porch by the hands of the apostles: 'And by the hands of the apostles were many signs and wonders wrought among the people; (and they were all with one accord in Solomon's porch . . . And believers were the more added to the Lord, multitudes both of men and women)' (5:12, 14).

The incident of the Lord Jesus in the temple recorded in John 10 falls naturally into four segments.

1. The challenge to the Lord by the Jews to declare plainly who He was (vv. 22-24)

'Then came the Jews round about him.' They surrounded the Lord and challenged Him: 'How long dost thou make us to doubt [hold us in suspense]? If thou be Christ, tell us plainly.'

Those who posed the question were probably not all

antagonistic to Him. Some were earnest enquirers, wondering if this could possibly be the Messiah. But what followed proved that some hated Him and they were waiting for Him to say something for which they could accuse Him.

2. *The answer given by the Lord to their challenge* (vv. 25-30)

In answer to their direct question the Lord spoke of His relationship with His Father.

Firstly, He says, 'The works that I do *in my Father's name*, they bear witness of me.' The miracles He performed, which they could not deny, were the authentication of His link with the Father.

Secondly, He speaks of His sheep (His people) as being a gift from His Father. '*My Father, which gave them me,* is greater than all.'

Thirdly, He speaks of the security of His own because they are in the hand of His Father. 'No man is able to pluck them out of *my Father's hand.*'

Fourthly, He affirms His oneness with the Father, '*I and my Father are one.*'

His answer to their question was unequivocal and unmistakable. He was claiming to be the Messiah, to be one with the Father; He was claiming to be God. Before the conversation ended He would state categorically, 'Say ye of Him, whom the Father hath sanctified, and sent into the world, Thou blasphemest; because I said, I am the Son of God?' Could there ever be a greater contrast than between Antiochus the wicked and Christ? Antiochus desecrated the brazen altar in the temple by offering a blasphemous sacrifice to the Greek god, Jupiter. He represented a false god; the Lord Jesus could say with absolute veracity, 'I am the Son of God.'

3. *The reaction of the Jewish leaders to His answer* (vv. 31-39)

The reaction of the Jewish leaders was to take up stones to stone Him. After further discussion we read, 'Therefore they sought again to take him: but he escaped out of their hand.' There had been a previous occasion at Nazareth, after His first public reading of Scripture: 'And all they in the synagogue, when they heard these things, were filled with wrath, And rose up, and thrust him out of the city, and led him unto the brow of the hill whereon their city was built, that they might cast him down headlong. But he passing through the midst of them went his way' (Luke 4:28-30). On both of these occasions we are reminded of the statement, repeated a number of times in John's Gospel, 'mine/his hour was not yet come' (2:4; 7:30; 8:20).

In this section the Lord Jesus makes more references to His Father: He was sent by the Father: 'Say ye of Him, whom the Father hath sanctified, and sent into the world . . .?'; 'If I do not the works of my Father, believe me not'; '. . . that ye may know, and believe, that the Father is in me, and I in Him.'

4. *The Lord leaving the city, and His destination* (vv. 40-42)

'And went away again beyond Jordan into the place where John at first baptized; and there he abode. And many resorted unto him . . . And many believed on Him there.'

A summary of some of the cardinal truths taught by the Lord Jesus in Solomon's porch

His deity: 'I am the Son of God' (v. 36).

His equality with the Father: 'I and my Father are one' (vv. 30, 38).

The security of His sheep: 'They shall never perish, neither shall any man pluck them out of my hand . . . no man is able to pluck them out of my Father's hand' (vv. 28-29).

The reliability of Scripture: 'The scripture cannot be broken' (v. 35).

'. . . in his temple doth everything speak of his glory' (Psalm 29:9). The Lord Jesus was walking in the temple; how significant it is, then, that He expressed these amazing truths concerning His deity and His equality with the Father.

CHAPTER 6

Stretching Out His Hand

1. To heal the sick

Peter's wife's mother: in Peter's house

'. . . they entered into the house of Simon and Andrew, with James and John. But Simon's wife's mother lay sick of a fever, and anon they tell him of her. And he came and took her by the hand, and lifted her up; and immediately the fever left her, and she ministered unto them' (Mark 1:29-31).

Having left the synagogue, the Lord Jesus came with some of His disciples into Simon's house. The favoured three, Simon, James and John, were all there. Simon's wife's mother was seriously ill. Her condition is described by Luke the physician as 'a great fever' (Luke 4:38). Soon after their arrival they told the Lord about her. Mark simply says, 'and anon they tell him of her' (1:30). In his account, Luke stresses the earnestness of their request: 'and they besought him for her' (v. 38).

What a great blessing for the Christian that, when illness comes, we can speak to the Lord about it. He is the great physician who never had to turn away anyone who came seeking healing. No case was beyond His ability to cure, no one ever had to be referred to someone else, and no one ever had to return for further treatment.

When Lazarus was sick at Bethany, his two sisters, Mary and Martha, sent a message to the Lord saying, 'He whom thou lovest is sick' (John 11:3). We have an even greater blessing in that we can speak directly to the Lord at all times. James tells us, 'the prayer of faith shall save the sick, and the Lord shall raise him up.' He continues, '. . . pray one for another, that ye may be healed' (James 5:15-16). We pray believing that God is able, but accepting His sovereign will.

We stand in awe of the amazing authority with which the Lord spoke. Luke says, 'And he stood over her, and *rebuked* the fever; and it left her' (Luke 4:39). Earlier He *rebuked* a demon and it came out (v. 35). Luke tells us, 'And they were all amazed, and spake among themselves, saying, What a word is this! for with authority and power he commanded the unclean spirits, and they come out' (v. 36). On the Sea of Galilee, when the storm raged, Luke records, 'And he arose, and *rebuked* the wind . . . (8:24).

Mark's account tells us, 'And he came and took her by the hand, and lifted her up; and immediately the fever left her, and she ministered unto them' (1:31). No convalescence was necessary; her strength was completely restored and immediately she was able to serve others.

A leper: in Galilee

'And there came a leper to him, beseeching him, and kneeling down to him, and saying unto him, If thou wilt, thou canst make me clean. And Jesus, moved with compassion, put forth his hand, and touched him, and saith unto him, I will;

be thou clean. And as soon as he had spoken, immediately the leprosy departed from him, and he was cleansed. And he straitly charged him, and forthwith sent him away; And saith unto him, See thou say nothing to any man: but go thy way, shew thyself to the priest, and offer for thy cleansing those things which Moses commanded, for a testimony unto them' (Mark 1:40-44).

In the midst of the Lord's busy service in Galilee, a leper came to Him, kneeling down and beseeching Him, saying, 'If Thou wilt, Thou canst make me clean.' According to the law, he ought to have remained at a distance; lepers were separated from society because of the contagious nature of the disease. They had to warn of their approach, shouting, 'Unclean, unclean!' (Lev. 13:45-46).

Luke the physician describes the condition of this man as being 'full of leprosy,' meaning that the disease was at an advanced stage. In spite of the seriousness of his condition, he was convinced that Christ was able to cure him. What he said to the Lord was, 'If You are willing, You are able to cleanse me.' The only doubt in his mind was, would He be willing? The Lord knew his condition, his sincerity, his humility and his faith. He stretched out His hand and touched him, and said, 'I will, be thou clean.'

The result was instantaneous: his leprosy was gone. The first thing that the Lord did was to touch the leper, which would have been the last thing others would have done. The risk of infection was high enough to keep most people at arm's length. Then there was the matter of being defiled by such contact, another reason to stay clear. As the healing of the leper was immediate, the question of defilement could not arise: there was no defilement from touching a leper who had been cleansed. Mark informs us that Jesus was moved with compassion towards him. Others avoided him, but the Lord of all touched him and met his need.

The Lord asked two things of the man. Firstly, that he would not tell anyone what had happened to him. Secondly, that he would go to the priest, to verify that he had been cleansed, and offer two birds as required by the law (Lev. 14:4). He failed to keep silent. 'But he went out, and began to publish it much, and to blaze abroad the matter.' The result was that that 'Jesus could no more openly enter into the city, but was without in desert places: and they came to him from every quarter' (Mark 1:45).

How wonderful to see the willingness of Christ to touch the leper and cleanse him. Still as of old, the Saviour is willing to receive us and cleanse us from the defilement of sin, if we come to Him in humility and faith, as the leper did so long ago. 'The blood of Jesus Christ his son cleanseth us from all sin' (1 John 1:7).

The deaf and dumb man: at the Sea of Galilee

This miracle is recorded only by Mark (7:31-37). The Lord Jesus had just arrived at the Sea of Galilee, having travelled from Tyre and Sidon. A deaf man, who also had a speech impediment, was brought by his friends to the Lord. They realized that no other physician was able to heal him and believed that Christ alone was able to meet the man's need. The text says, 'they beseech him to put his hand upon him' (v. 32). These friends were earnest; they were pleading with the Lord to help the deaf man. We too have the privilege of speaking directly to the Lord, interceding for our friends and loved ones who need the salvation which He alone can give.

The Lord acted promptly in response to their request (v. 33). 'And he took him aside from the multitude, and put his fingers into his ears, and he spit, and touched his tongue; And looking up to heaven, he sighed, and saith unto him, Ephphatha, that is, Be opened.' Why did He sigh? Standing before him was a man whose condition resulted from the entrance into the world of sin, bringing in its wake disease, and death. Here was One who not only felt the tragedy of the Fall, but He was able to meet the man's need. The Lord touched both his ears and his tongue, 'And straightway his ears were opened, and the string of his tongue was loosed, and he spake plain' (v. 35). The result was immediate healing for both ailments.

How wonderful is the immediacy of God's offer of salvation! A person may have wasted years of life ignoring the claims of Christ, yet, if they repent and believe on the Lord Jesus, He saves immediately. This in no way affects the urgency of the matter of salvation. Scripture still says, 'Now is the accepted time' (2 Cor. 6:2). The fact is, we have no guarantee of tomorrow and no assurance that we will repent at some future time. Scripture records of Esau, '. . . he was rejected: for he found no place of repentance, though he sought it carefully with tears' (Heb.12:17).

Not only was the miracle immediate, but the healing was complete: 'His ears were opened . . . and he spake plain.' Those who witnessed it, 'published it; And were beyond measure astonished, saying, He hath done all things well: He maketh both the deaf to hear, and the dumb to speak' (v. 37).

The blind man: at Bethsaida

As with the previous miracle, the healing of the blind man

at Bethsaida is recorded only in Mark's Gospel (8:22-26). There are parallels in the two passages. The blind man also had friends who brought him to the Lord Jesus. Again they ask the Lord to touch him, and again He takes the man away from the multitude: 'He took the blind man by the hand, and led him out of the town' (v. 23).

Picture the scene. The blind man is striding purposefully along the road out of town. If you could ask him, 'Are you not afraid of stumbling? After all, you can't see the road ahead,' he would reply, 'Do you not see who is holding my hand? It is Jesus of Nazareth. I am safe, for He is by my side.' Again, you might ask him, 'Do you know where you are going?' and his answer would be, 'No, but I trust the One who holds me with His hand; He knows the way.' When they were outside the town the Lord spat on his eyes, and put His hands upon him. He then asked the blind man if he saw anything. 'And he looked up, and said, I see men as trees, walking. After that he put his hands again upon his eyes, and made him look up: and he was restored, and saw every man clearly' (vv. 24-25).

In both of these miracles the healing was complete. The dumb man spoke plainly (7:35), and the blind man saw clearly (8:25). Firstly, the Lord spat on his eyes. Had he applied some ointment from the local apothecary, the sceptics would have said, 'Wasn't that ointment wonderful? What an amazing result!' But in both cases, the healing must all be attributed to Christ and to Christ alone.

Why did the healing of the blind man seem to be progressive and not instantaneous? This miracle illustrates that sometimes spiritual enlightenment is progressive. We do not see everything clearly at first; a measure of blindness still remains until the light ultimately dawns upon the soul. The Lord Jesus is not only the author but also the finisher of our faith. There is no doubt whatever that the new birth takes place in a moment, yet up to that moment there may be a gradual learning and appreciation of the truth.

The multitude: at Capernaum

'Now when the sun was setting, all they that had any sick with divers diseases brought them unto him; and he laid his hands on every one of them, and healed them' (Luke 4:40).

We watch the untiring patience of the great Physician at the close of a busy day. A great crowd of sick folk had been brought by their friends to the Master.

Mark informs us, 'all the city was gathered together at the door' (1:33). Luke says, 'and he laid his hands on every one of them, and healed them.' The One we have considered, who healed the different individuals and countless others as well, was able to meet the needs of the multitude, one by one.

> *At even, ere the sun was set,*
> *The sick, O Lord, around Thee lay;*
> *O in what divers pains they met!*
> *O with what joy they went away!*
>
> *Thy touch has still its ancient power;*
> *No word from Thee can fruitless fall:*
> *Hear, in this solemn evening hour,*
> *And in Thy mercy heal us all.*
>
> Henry Twells

Malchus: in Gethsemane

This is the last recorded healing miracle performed by the Lord Jesus (Luke 22:50-51). It took place in the garden of Gethsemane. In the darkness, the disciples must have been terrified to see the flickering lights and the emerging band of men, 'with lanterns and torches and weapons' (John 18:3). Mark speaks of 'a great multitude' (14:43). How ludicrous that so many, with such an array of weapons, were deployed to arrest one man. At the head of that motley crew was Judas Iscariot, 'one of the twelve.'

Impetuous as ever, Peter drew his sword and struck the high priest's servant, cutting off his ear. Some of the disciples had asked, 'Lord, shall we smite with the sword?' (Luke 22:49), but Peter didn't wait for the answer. With only two swords between them (v. 38), how did he think that he and the other disciples could protect the Lord from a great multitude? He acted hastily and didn't stop to think.

Luke gives us details which the other Gospel writers omit. He says it was his right ear, and he alone mentions the healing. John refers to a disciple who was known to the high priest (18:15). This was probably himself, and perhaps the reason why he alone knew the servant's name: 'The servant's name was Malchus' (v. 10). Peter would doubtless have gone further but for the words of Christ, 'Put up thy sword into the sheath: the cup which my Father hath given me, shall I not drink it?' (v. 11).

The chief priests and elders may have sent a great multitude, but the Lord spoke to Peter of a far greater host who would readily have come to His aid, if called upon. 'Thinkest thou that

I cannot now pray to my Father, and he shall presently give me more than twelve legions of angels? [more than 72,000]. But how then shall the scriptures be fulfilled, that thus it must be?' (Matt. 26:53-54). He also spoke to the multitude about the fulfilment of Scripture. 'Are ye come out against a thief with swords and staves for to take me? I sat daily with you teaching in the temple, and ye laid no hold on me. But all this was done that the scriptures of the prophets might be fulfilled' (vv. 55-56).

The miracle of the healing of Malchus is unique in Scripture. The Lord Jesus is seen not only as Healer but as Creator. He was able to recreate the portion of the ear that had been cut off and heal the man completely. It is also the only recorded miracle of healing where the wound had been caused by violence.

The healing was brought about by His touch. 'And he touched his ear, and healed him' (Luke 22:51). What a contrast when we consider the action of Peter, '[He] stretched out his hand, and drew his sword' (Matt. 26:51). The Lord Jesus stretched out His hand to heal; Peter stretched out his hand to harm. Peter would later reflect on this incident and write, 'When he suffered, he threatened not' (1 Pet. 2:23). What an example the Lord was of His own teaching: 'But love your enemies, and do good' (Luke 6:35). The final miracle before He died was for the healing of an enemy.

His suffering and death on the cross would provide a means whereby enemies can be reconciled to God. 'For if, when we were enemies, we were reconciled to God by the death of his Son . . .' (Rom. 5:10). What wondrous grace.

The healing of Malchus completely removed the evidence of a crime. Peter could have been charged with 'grievous bodily harm', or its equivalent in those days. After all, there were plenty of witnesses. But, while there were many witnesses, there was no evidence. The wound to Malchus' ear had been healed perfectly and no trace of the injury inflicted by Peter's sword remained.

What a wonderful picture of the believer's justification. Such is the eternal value of the work of Christ at Calvary that, when we receive Him by faith, the evidence of our sins is removed for ever from before the face of God. 'I, even I, am he that blotted out thy transgressions for mine own sake, and will not remember thy sins' (Isa. 43:25). 'There is therefore now no condemnation to them which are in Christ Jesus . . .' (Rom. 8:1).

2. To restore life

The widow of Nain's son: outside the city

The story begins with the Lord leaving Capernaum and coming to a city called Nain (Luke 7:11-17). As He and His disciples approach the city, there was a crowd of people with them— '. . . many of his disciples went with him, and much people' (v. 11).

As they come near to the gate of Nain, they meet a funeral possession coming out of the city. The funeral was of a young man; his heartbroken mother accompanied the coffin, 'and much people of the city was with her' (v. 12).

So two crowds of people meet: one going into the city and one coming out. This was no accidental meeting; it was in the providence of God that the large number would witness the amazing miracle soon to take place.

There were additional circumstances that added to the

mother's grief. The dead man was her 'only son', the one she would naturally look to for support in her old age; she was 'a widow', with no husband to comfort and support her in her trial; the Lord addressed him as '*Young* man'. Zechariah speaks of the intensity of grief for an only son: '. . . and they shall mourn for him, as one mourneth for his only son . . .' (12:10).

What compassion was expressed in the words of the Lord Jesus, 'Weep not.' It was not merely a request for the distraught woman to stop crying, but because He was just about to remove the cause of all her grief. 'And he came and touched the bier: and they that bare him stood still.' He then spoke to the young man: 'Young man, I say unto thee, Arise. And he that was dead sat up, and began to speak. And he delivered him to his mother' (vv. 13-15). There was no need for the Lord to fear ceremonial defilement, as the Jewish leaders would have done. At His touch and by His word, death fled instantaneously and its defilement was no more.

While the miracle was an act of compassion towards the bereaved woman, it was also a demonstration of His omnipotent power as God. '. . . that we should not trust in ourselves, but in God which raiseth the dead' (2 Cor. 1:9). 'Why should it be thought a thing incredible with you, that God should raise the dead?' (Acts 26:8). He was not raising the dead by delegated power, as Elijah and Elisha were. As God, all power belonged to Him.

Jairus' daughter: in the house

After the Lord Jesus had freed the man possessed by an unclean spirit in the country of the Gadarenes, He travelled by ship to the other side of the Sea of Galilee.

While He was on the shore, Jairus, a ruler of the synagogue, came and fell at His feet. 'My little daughter lieth at the point of death: I pray thee, come and lay thy hands on her, that she may be healed; and she shall live' (Mark 5:23). Matthew adds that he worshipped Him (9:18).

He came with humility: he fell at His feet; he came offering homage: he worshipped Him; he came with hope: he besought Him greatly; he came in faith: 'lay thy hands upon her, that she may be healed; and she shall live.'

The story is remarkable, in that Jairus was a prominent Jew, a ruler of the synagogue. Not many men in that position had any time for the Saviour. John comments, '. . . his own received him not' (1:11). Jairus had heard of the miracles which the Lord had performed and the blessing many had received. He believed implicitly that He would be able to heal his little daughter, who was so desperately ill and hovering at the very point of death. He realized that neither his position nor his wealth could avail anything to help his child. Christ alone could meet the need.

The Lord Jesus agreed to accompany him to his house, but as they commenced the journey, much to the frustration of Jairus, their progress was halted. A woman who had suffered for twelve years with an issue of blood came behind the Lord Jesus and touched the hem of His garment. Undetected by anyone in the crowd except the Lord, she was immediately healed. 'And Jesus, immediately knowing in himself that virtue had gone out of him, . . . said, Who touched my clothes?' (Mark 5:30). The woman fell down before Him in fear and trembling, 'And he said unto her, Daughter, thy faith hath made the whole; go in peace, and be whole of thy plague' (v. 34).

The woman had twelve years of suffering until she met the Saviour; Jairus had experienced twelve years of joy in the life of his little daughter. At that point, while Jesus was still speaking, messengers arrived from Jairus' house, bringing the sad news of his daughter's death: 'Thy daughter is dead: why troublest thou the Master any further?' (v. 35). But as soon as the Lord Jesus heard their message, He said, 'Be not afraid, only believe.' At that moment there were no grounds for optimism. The message was stark, 'Thy daughter is dead.' But the Lord said, 'Be not afraid, only believe' (v. 36).

At times, many of us may feel like the man who said with tears, 'Lord, I believe; help thou mine unbelief' (9:24).

Begone unbelief,
My Saviour is near,
And for my relief
Will surely appear:
By prayer let me wrestle,
And He will perform:
With Christ in the vessel,
I smile at the storm.

His love in time past
Forbids me to think
He'll leave me at last
In trouble to sink.
While each Ebenezer
I have in review
Confirms His good pleasure
To help me quite through.

John Newton

When they arrived at the house where the child was, the Lord took Peter, James and John with Him and they went in. A crowd had gathered, who 'wept and wailed greatly' v. 38. He said, 'Why make ye this ado, and weep? the damsel is not dead, but sleepeth.' Verse 40 says that they laughed Him to scorn. They knew nothing of the lovely simile that the Lord was using, speaking of death as *sleep*. He said concerning Lazarus, 'Our friend Lazarus sleepeth' (John 11:11). It says of Stephen, the first recorded martyr, as he was being stoned, 'he kneeled down, and cried with a loud voice, Lord, lay not this sin to their charge. And when he had said this, he fell asleep' (Acts 7:60).

So the Lord put them all out except the child's parents and Peter, James and John. Unbelief had no place in His presence. 'And when he was come into his own country . . . he did not many mighty works there because of their unbelief' (Matt. 13:54, 58). 'And he took the damsel by the hand, and said unto her, Talitha cumi; which is, being interpreted, Damsel, I say unto thee, arise. And straightway the damsel arose, and walked; for she was of the age of twelve years. And they were astonished . . .' (Mark 5:41-42). He took her cold little hand in His, and Luke the physician says that at the sound of His voice, 'her spirit came again' (Luke 8:55).

The Lord made two requests. Firstly, that they would tell no one; secondly, that they should give the child something to eat. When a person is born again, they are in need of spiritual sustenance: 'As new-born babes, desire the sincere milk of the word, that ye may grow thereby' (1 Pet. 2:2).

These two miracles, placed by Mark one within the other, have one thing in common: it was contact with Christ that brought blessing. The woman stooped down and touched the hem of His garment; He took Jairus' daughter by the hand and restored her life.

3. To bless the children: at the coasts of Judaea

'And they brought young children to him, that he should touch them: and his disciples rebuked those that brought them. But when Jesus saw it, he was much displeased, and said unto them, Suffer the little children to come unto me, and forbid them not: for of such is the kingdom of God. Verily I say unto you, Whosoever shall not receive the kingdom of God as a little child, he shall not enter therein. And he took them up in his arms, put his hands upon them, and blessed them' (Mark 10:13-16).

The place where this incident took place is identified as 'the coasts of Judaea by the farther side of Jordan' (v. 1). Parents brought their children, asking the Lord to touch them. They believed that by bringing them to Him the children would be blessed. There is no more noble desire that parents could have for their children, than one by one they might come to know Christ. Therein lies the secret of happiness in this life and a blessed assurance of Heaven in the world to come. Moses wrote, 'O satisfy us early with thy mercy; that we may rejoice and be glad all our days' (Ps. 90:14). This Psalm has the title, 'A prayer of Moses the man of God.'

The words used by Mark indicate that the children were very young: 'young children, little children' (vv. 13-14). I write these words with the joy of hearing just yesterday of a little girl of four who confessed Christ as her Saviour, having attended the children's meeting.

By using both a positive and a negative statement, the

Master made clear His willingness to welcome children who come to Him: 'Suffer the little children to come unto me, and forbid them not.' He also gives us the reason why: 'for of such is the kingdom of God.' Everyone who arrives safely in Heaven may not have been saved as a child, but all were saved by simple faith in Christ. It is a true saying, 'It's not a childish thing to be saved, but it can only be received in childlike faith.' The words of the Lord Jesus are, 'Whosoever shall not receive the kingdom of God as a little child, he shall not enter therein' (v. 15).

Opposition came from an unexpected quarter: 'his disciples rebuked those who brought them.' They either considered that the Lord was too busy, or the children were too young. The Scripture says, 'But when Jesus saw it, he was much displeased . . . And he took them up in his arms, put his hands upon them, and blessed them' (vv. 14, 16). He took time to bless them one by one. This was the One of whom Isaiah wrote, 'He shall gather the lambs with his arm' (Isa. 40:11). We can safely conclude that, just as the Lord was 'much displeased' by those who sought to hinder the children, He is pleased with those who use their best efforts to bring them to Him.

> *I think when I read that sweet story of old,*
> *When Jesus was here among men,*
> *How He called little children as lambs to His fold,*
> *I should like to have been with them then.*
>
> *In that beautiful place He has gone to prepare*
> *For all who are washed and forgiven,*
> *Many dear children are gathering there,*
> *For of such is the kingdom of Heaven.*
>
> Jemima Luke

4. To bless the disciples: at Bethany

'And he led them out as far as to Bethany, and he lifted up his hands, and blessed them. And it came to pass, while he blessed them, he was parted from them, and carried up into heaven' (Luke 24:50-51).

'And when he had spoken these things, while they beheld, he was taken up; and a cloud received him out of their sight. And while they looked stedfastly toward heaven as he went up, behold, two men stood by them in white apparel' (Acts 1:9-10).

These are the two historical accounts given by Luke of the ascension. The only other one was written by Mark: 'So then after the Lord had spoken unto them, he was received up into heaven, and sat on the right hand of God' (16:19).

Luke identifies for us the place from which the Lord ascended as 'the mount called Olivet' (Acts 1:12). He adds a more precise location on the mountain in his Gospel: 'And he led them out as far as to Bethany' (24:50). The last action He performed on earth was to lift up His hands, and the last words He spoke on earth were words of blessing.

The Prophecy of Malachi concludes with a call to repentance, 'lest I come and smite the earth with a curse' (Mal. 4:6), making 'curse' the last word in our Old Testament. Nevertheless, the promise had been given to Abraham, 'in thee shall all families of the earth be blessed' (Gen. 12:3), and the Lord Jesus came as the fulfilment of that promise.

The first verse of our New Testament states clearly that what follows is, 'The book of the generation of Jesus Christ, the son of David, the son of Abraham' (Matt. 1:1). Right on the threshold of the New Testament the Messiah is introduced to us as the One who would bring the promised blessing by His birth, His life, His death and His resurrection. After His resurrection the Apostles preached a message that brought blessing into the lives of those who received it: 'Unto you first God, having raised up his Son Jesus, sent him to bless you, in turning away every one of you from his iniquities' (Acts 3:26).

Luke states, 'He was parted from them' (Luke 24:51). From that moment onward until He returns again, the Lord is absent from His people. He often told His disciples that the day would come when He must leave them. '. . . I go to prepare a place for you. And if I go and prepare a place for you, I will come again, and receive you unto myself' (John 14:2-3). We live today during the time of His absence, but we await the moment of His return.

In Acts 1:9 the emphasis is different, He is out of sight: '. . . a cloud received him out of their sight.' Peter writes, 'Whom having not seen, ye love' (1 Peter 1:8). Again, the Lord had forewarned His disciples that that day would come. 'A little while, and ye shall not see me: and again, a little while, and ye shall see me, because I go to the Father' (John 16:16). To His people today, our Lord Jesus is both absent and out of sight. He can only be known by faith.

The Lord was in the act of blessing the disciples when He began to ascend. They watched Him go until a cloud received Him out of their sight. While He was blessing them He was parted from them, but blessing His own did not finish when He left them. The lesson for us is that He is still engaged in blessing His people from Heaven. He is our great high priest, our advocate with the Father. His work on the cross is gloriously complete, but His work on the throne is an unfinished work that will continue until He comes again.

He bears the wonderful title, 'A minister of the sanctuary' (Heb. 8:2). 'But now hath he obtained a more excellent ministry' (v. 6). His place of service is now above, where He is engaged in working for our blessing.

He is our Intercessor. 'Wherefore he is able also to save them to the uttermost that come unto God by him, seeing he ever liveth to make intercession for them' (Heb. 7:25). To erring Peter, He said, 'Satan hath desired to have you, that he may sift you as wheat: But I have prayed for thee, that thy faith fail not' (Luke 22:31-32). Doubtless, we benefit daily from the constancy of His intercession.

He is our advocate with the Father. 'And if any man sin, we have an advocate with the Father, Jesus Christ the righteous' (1 John 2:1). He is the One who can restore our communion with the Father when this has been temporarily lost because of sin. 'If we confess our sins, he is faithful and just to forgive us our sins, and to cleanse us from all unrighteousness' (1 John 1:9).

He is our great high priest. As he went into the holy place, the high priest of old carried the name of each of the twelve tribes of Israel on his shoulders and on his breastplate. A unique stone was associated with each tribe. Two stones represented each tribe: one on the shoulder piece, the place of strength; one on the breastplate, the place of affection. Our high priest is able to support us in our frailty and carry our burdens.

The stones on the shoulders of the high priest were called 'stones of memorial'. 'Aaron shall bear their names before the Lord upon his two shoulders for a memorial . . . And Aaron shall bear the names of the children of Israel in the breastplate of judgment upon his heart, when he goeth in unto the holy place, for a memorial before the Lord continually' (Ex. 28:12, 29).

'Cast thy burden upon the Lord, and he shall sustain thee' (Ps. 55:22). He knows (John 21:17); He cares (1 Pet. 5:7); He feels (Heb. 4:15); He succours (Heb. 2:18). What a wonderful reassurance the believer has today: the One who died to save us, lives to bless us. Whatever trial we pass through, He knows. Not only does He know, but He cares. Not only does He know and care, but He feels for us. Not only does He know and care and feel for us, but He is able to succour (draw alongside to help).

> *Before the throne of God above,*
> *I have a strong and perfect plea,*
> *A great High Priest whose name is Love,*
> *Who ever lives and pleads for me.*
>
> Charitie Lees Bancroft

CHAPTER 7

Bowing His Head

'He bowed his head' (John 19:30). We stand on holy ground as we consider those sacred moments which immediately preceded the death of Christ at Calvary. John tells us of His penultimate cry from the cross, 'It is finished.' Matthew, Mark and Luke each inform us that the cry was 'with a loud voice' (Matthew 27:50; Mark 15:37; Luke 23:46.)

It was not a feeble almost inaudible whisper spoken in weakness by a dying man; it was a mighty cry of victory that would reverberate throughout earth and heaven. Believers would rejoice in it, angels would wonder at it, and the demons would tremble on hearing it.

The order of events is clear: 'He bowed his head, and gave up the spirit.' He was in control: it was not an involuntary result of His death that His head inclined on His breast, but rather His last recorded action. He bowed His head and said, 'Father, into thy hands I commend my spirit' (Luke 23:46.)

Death had no claim upon Him as it has on all others— 'For the wages of sin is death' (Rom. 6:23.) He was the spotless, unblemished Lamb of God. His death was voluntary in the absolute sense, not merely that He allowed men to crucify Him. He said, 'No man taketh [my life] from me, but I lay it down of myself. I have power to lay it down, and I have power to take it again. This commandment have I received of my Father' (John 10:18). It is not therefore correct ever to speak of Christ as 'a dying man'. When the Scriptures were fulfilled and His work was finished He, who is the 'Prince of life', was 'obedient unto [to the point of] death, even the death of the cross' (Phil. 2:8).

No other person could *commend* his spirit to God. Everything concerning Christ—whether thought or word or deed—was commendable and brought delight to the heart of God. David said, 'Into thine hand I *commit* my spirit' (Ps. 31:5). Stephen, the first recorded martyr, said as he was dying, 'Lord Jesus, *receive* my spirit' (Acts 7:59). As in many other aspects of His birth, life, death and resurrection, Christ is unique; and also in this— the manner in which He commended His spirit to His Father. The word *klino*, which is translated 'bowed' here, is translated elsewhere in various ways which are rich in meaning when related to our text.

We will consider how it is rendered in three other passages.

1. In Matthew 8:20, when seeking to dissuade would-be followers, who had not stopped to consider the cost of discipleship, the Lord Jesus said, 'Foxes have holes, and the birds of the air have nests; but the Son of man hath not where to lay his head.' The words 'to lay' are a translation of the word *klino*. The one for whom no room was found and had on earth nowhere to lay His head, at last bowed His head upon His own breast and commended His spirit to His Father.

Here we are reminded of the circumstances of poverty into which the Lord Jesus was born and in which He lived. '… for your sakes he became poor, that ye through his poverty might be rich' (2 Cor. 8:9). When He bowed His head on the cross, His shame, His poverty and His humiliation were forever past.

Soon His body would be anointed with 'a mixture of myrrh and aloes, about an hundred pound weight,' brought by Nicodemus. Soon His body would be laid in the rock hewn tomb in the garden, donated by a rich man, Joseph of Arimathaea. Soon His body would be watched over by angels, one at His head and another at His feet. The words of Isaiah written many centuries before His birth were fulfilled, '[He was] with the rich in His death' (53:9).

2. The same word *(klino)* occurs in Hebrews 11:34 concerning the heroes of faith, who 'turned to fight the armies of the aliens.' The words 'turned to flight' are a translation of *klino*.

When the Lord Jesus bowed His head it was a visible sign of a great victory won, enemies being put to flight, and every foe defeated. 'And having spoiled principalities and powers, he made a show of them openly, triumphing over them in it' (Col. 2:15); '… that through death he might destroy him that had the power of death, that is, the devil' (Heb. 2:14).

The believer enters into the good of the victory won at the cross. Just as the children of Israel entered into the good of David's victory when Goliath was slain in the valley of Elah (1 Sam. 17), so Paul reminds us that 'we are more than conquerors through him that loved us' (Rom. 8:37).

> *How hast Thou triumphed, and triumphed with glory,*
> *Battled death's forces, rolled back every wave!*
> *Can we refrain then from telling the story,*
> *How Thou art victor o'er death and the grave?*
>
> H. d'A. Champney

3. Another occurrence of *klino* is in Luke 24:29, where we read, '… the day is *far spent.*' When the Lord bowed His head it brought to an end His day of service on earth. What a day of service it was: from early boyhood, when His first recorded words were, '. . . I must be about my Father's business' (Luke 2:49), until at last He could testify to His Father, 'I have glorified thee on the earth: I have finished the work which thou gavest me to do' (John 17:4).

He is the perfect servant of Jehovah. Every moment of every day was filled with busy service for God. He was the only servant who could truthfully say, 'I do always those things that please him' (John 8:29).

Seven Miracles

At the precise moment that the Lord Jesus bowed His head and dismissed His spirit, *seven miracles occurred simultaneously.* This is made clear in Matthew 27:50-52, which mentions five of them: 'Jesus, when he had cried again with a loud voice, yielded up the ghost. And, behold, the veil of the temple was rent in twain from the top to the bottom; and the earth did quake, and the rocks rent; And the graves were opened.'

Mark records the sixth: 'And when the centurion, which stood over against him, saw that he so cried out, and gave up the ghost, he said, Truly this man was the Son of God' (15:39).

The seventh miracle was the darkness, which had occurred at midday. 'And when the sixth hour was come, there was darkness over the whole land until the ninth hour' (v. 33). When the Lord Jesus bowed His head and dismissed His spirit, the darkness was dispelled and the sun shed its light throughout the land once more.

1. The miracle of the Saviour's death: He yielded up His own spirit.

2. The miracle in the sanctuary: the veil was rent.

3. The miracle in the subterranean realm: the earth did quake.

4. The miracle in the stones: the rocks rent.

5. The miracle in the sepulchres: the graves were opened.

6. The miracle in a sinner's heart: the centurion believed.

7. The miracle in the sky: the sun was darkened

The miracle of the Saviour's death

The Oxford English Dictionary defines *miracle* as, 'an extraordinary and welcome event that is not explicable by natural or scientific laws and is therefore attributed to a divine agency.'

The death of the Saviour at Calvary was a miracle

No other person could claim that his or her death was miraculous. Death is inescapable for all mankind; an appointment that cannot be avoided. Some may speak of an accident being averted, or recovery from a serious illness as a miraculous escape from death, but for us death itself is no miracle.

Solomon said, 'There is no man that hath power over the spirit to retain the spirit; neither hath he power in the day of death' (Eccl. 8:8). Only the Lord Jesus had such power. He said, 'No man taketh [my life] from me, but I lay it down of myself. I have power to lay it down, and I have power to take it again' (John 10:18). The choice He made was not between dying at one time rather than another, but between dying or not dying.

The death of Christ was miraculous because it was voluntary

It is true that Peter, speaking on the day of Pentecost, charged the men of Israel with His death: 'Him . . . ye have taken, and by wicked hands have crucified and slain' (Acts 2:23). Again, outside the temple after the healing of the lame man, he said, 'But ye denied the Holy One and the Just … and killed the Prince of life' (3:14-15). To the high priest, Peter further says, 'The God of our fathers raised up Jesus, whom ye slew and hanged on a tree' (5:30). The Jews and the Romans were therefore morally responsible for the death of Christ. They must bear 'the guilt of innocent blood' (Deut. 19:13).

In spite of the cruelty and barbarity of those who were responsible for His crucifixion, the Lord Jesus did not die from natural causes. When the Scriptures had been fulfilled, when the mighty ransom price had been paid and the enemy had been defeated, He commended His Spirit to His Father.

The death of Christ was miraculous because of who He was

The man who died on the centre cross was 'the Son of God' (Gal. 2:20). God cannot die: He is 'the high and lofty One that inhabiteth eternity, whose name is Holy' (Isa. 57:15)—but, wonder of wonders, the Son of God became man so that He might die on the cross. 'But we see Jesus, who was made a little lower than the angels *for the suffering of death*, crowned with glory and honour; that he by the grace of God should taste death for every man' (Heb. 2:9).

At Bethlehem God was not born, but the One who was born was God.

At Calvary God did not die, but the One who died was God.

The miracle in the sanctuary

Adam and Eve were driven out of the Garden of Eden because of sin. The access to God's presence that they had once enjoyed was now denied.

When the tabernacle was set up, there was a veil erected between the holy place and the holiest of all. The reason for this is, 'The Holy Spirit this signifying, that the way into the holiest of all was not yet made manifest' (Heb. 9:8). Only the high priest could enter there on one day of the year, the Day of Atonement, and 'not without blood' (v. 7).

Hebrews 10:19-20 speaks of the believer today, 'having . . . boldness to enter into the holiest by the blood of Jesus. By a new and living way, which he hath consecrated for us, through the veil, that is to say, his flesh.' The veil represents the perfect life of Christ in the days of His flesh. His sinless life alone could never save us. On the contrary, it further emphasizes how far we fall short of the divine standard. The unrent veil stood as a barrier separating sinful man from a holy God.

At the precise moment that the Lord Jesus bowed His head and dismissed His spirit, 'the veil of the temple was rent in twain from the top to the bottom' (Matt. 27:51); and 'rent in the midst' (Luke 23:45). It was torn into two pieces, completely severed from the top to the bottom; torn in the midst, or centrally, allowing full access between the holy place and the holiest of all. The rending of the veil was complete.

The fact that the veil was torn from the top indicates that it was the work of God. We should revel in the fact that believers now have access at all times into God's immediate presence, to come with our confession, prayers and worship. But we should always remember the tremendous cost by which this liberty has been won, 'by the blood of Jesus' (Heb. 10:19); and by His body given in death upon the cross. When instituting the Lord's Supper, the Lord Jesus said, 'Take, eat: this is my body, which is [given] for you' (1 Cor. 11:24). In John 6:51 He said, '… the bread that I will give is my flesh, which I will give for the life of the world.'

> *Through Thy precious body broken*
> *Inside the veil;*
> *O what words to sinners spoken,*
> *Inside the veil;*
> *Precious as the blood that bought us,*
> *Perfect as the love that sought us,*
> *Holy as the Lamb that brought us*
> *Inside the veil.*
>
> Elizabeth Dark

The miracle in the subterranean realm

The two most momentous events in the history of this world were closely followed by earthquakes:

'… the earth did quake' (Matt 27:51). This was immediately following the death of Christ, and was creation's response to the death of the great Creator.

Immediately after our Lord's resurrection, we read, 'And, behold, there was a great earthquake' (28:2).

Most of those who were in the vicinity of Calvary were completely ignorant of who the man on the centre cross actually was, and they had no understanding of what the implications of His death were for them. How amazing, therefore, that the inanimate creation made such a tangible and dramatic display to mark the event. 'Then the earth shook and trembled; the foundations of heaven moved and shook, because he was wroth' (2 Sam 22:8). This scripture indicates that earthquakes often indicate God's wrath. At Calvary, God's Son bore the wrath of God so that we might 'be saved from wrath through him' (Rom. 5:9). The resurrection assures the believer that the question of sin and judgment has been settled: 'Who was delivered for our offences, and was raised again for our justification' (Rom. 4:25).

The jailor at Philippi could have testified that the Lord used an earthquake to bring him to the point of repentance, when he cried out, 'What must I do to be saved?' (Acts 16:26-30).

Believers can trace the basis of all their hopes to two great events, each of which, as a mark of their significance, was accompanied by an earthquake.

The miracle in the stones

To the passer-by, the scene at Calvary appeared to be one of weakness and defeat. But at the precise moment that the Lord Jesus bowed His head and dismissed His Spirit there was, in the rending of the rocks, a remarkable demonstration of His almighty power.

121

Rock is the hardest, most durable, natural material; yet, without any human force, the record of Scripture states, 'the rocks rent' (Matt. 27:51). The miracle was in the fact that the rocks imploded. It was not as a result of an external force, but they imploded from within. The power of God was at work. The significance of the words lies in the fact that they give a preview of the great blessing yet to be realized by creation because of the value of the work of the cross. Not only did the Lord Jesus die for everyone, but also for everything: '. . . that by the grace of God he should taste death for everything' (Heb. 2:9 JND).

'Yet once more I shake not the earth only, but also heaven. And this word, Yet once more, signified the removing of those things that are [may be] shaken . . . that those things which cannot be shaken may remain. Wherefore we receiving a kingdom which cannot be moved, let us have grace, whereby we may serve God acceptably with reverence and godly fear' (Heb. 12:26-28; cf Haggai 2:6).

Everything visible and tangible is temporary. One day the heavens and the earth will be changed, and the new heavens and earth will emerge (2 Pet. 3:10-13). What a day that will be, when every trace of the Fall will be removed forever because of the triumphs of Calvary. Praise God, we have an unshakable kingdom.

> *Thy sympathies and hopes are ours:*
> *We long, O Lord, to see*
> *Creation all — below, above,*
> *Redeemed and blessed by Thee.*
>
> Edward Denny

The miracle in the sepulchres

At the precise moment that the Lord Jesus dismissed His

Spirit on the cross, yet another miracle took place: 'And the graves were opened; and many bodies of the saints which slept arose, And came out of the graves after his resurrection, and went into the holy city, and appeared unto many' (Matt 27:52-53).

Questions arise: 1. How many of the saints arose? 2. With what bodies did they rise? 3. How long did they live before they died again? These are matters on which the Scriptures are silent and it is therefore fruitless for us to speculate as to what the answers might be.

The Lord Jesus has the pre-eminence in all things. In these verses we are told that the saints which slept arose, and came out of the graves *after His resurrection*. Others had been raised from the dead in both the Old and New Testaments, but, to this point, He alone arose, never to die again.

The resurrection of these saints was a proclamation of the great victory which had been won at Calvary: 'that through death he might destroy him that had the power of death, that is, the devil' (Heb. 2:14). It points forward to a day of ultimate victory when, in resurrection, every saint shall be beyond the power of death at last: '. . . then shall be brought to pass the saying that is written, Death is swallowed up in victory. O death, where is thy sting? O grave, where is thy victory?' (1 Cor. 15: 54-55).

It was a preview of the glorious morning when the Lord shall come to the air with a quickening shout, and every sleeping saint will hear His voice and be raised and changed and glorified in a moment of time (1 Thess. 4:15-17).

David's prospect for the future contrasts with that of the

man of the world: 'I shall be satisfied, when I awake, with thy likeness' (Ps. 17:15).

> *Oh, what a meeting, there in the skies;*
> *No tears nor crying shall dim our eyes.*
> *Loved ones united eternally,*
> *Oh, what a daybreak that morn shall be.*
>
> C. Blackmore

The miracle in a sinner's heart

Three Gospel writers mention the centurion who was in charge of the crucifixion: Matthew, Mark and Luke.

Matthew informs us that his duty entailed 'watching Jesus' (27:54).

Mark points out how near he stood to the cross, 'which stood over against him' (15:39). He was close enough to read the sign that Pilate had fixed over the cross, 'Jesus of Nazareth, the King of the Jews' (John 19:19). He would have known the significance of the name 'Jesus'—the Saviour, and he heard the taunting of some who passed by the cross saying, 'He saved others; himself he cannot save' (Mark 15:31).

Luke shows that the centurion was near enough to hear the words spoken by the Lord on the cross: 'Father, forgive them; for they know not what they do' (23:34). He would also have heard His cry of abandonment, 'My God, My God, why hast thou forsaken me?' (Matt. 27:46), and His reassuring word to the repentant malefactor, 'Today shalt thou be with me in paradise' (Luke 23:43). What impressed him most of all was the manner in which the Lord Jesus bowed His head, and said, 'Father, into thy hands I commend my spirit' (v. 46).

The miracles which followed—the darkness, the earthquake, the rending of the stones—these were visible, tangible and audible signs to convince even the most sceptical.

He feared God. '. . . the centurion, and they that were with him . . . feared greatly (Matt. 27:54). Earlier, he had heard the malefactor ask his companion, 'Dost not thou fear God?' (Luke 23:40).

He glorified God. For the first time in his life, the words that the centurion spoke brought glory to God: 'He glorified God, saying, Certainly this was a righteous man' (v. 47). Earlier, he had heard the malefactor say, 'This man hath done nothing amiss' (v. 41), and it dawned upon him that the One on the centre cross was not there for crimes which He Himself had committed.

He confessed Christ to be the Son of God. 'Truly this was the Son of God' (Matt 27:54); 'Truly this man was the Son of God' (Mark 15:39).

He confirmed to Pilate that Christ was dead. 'And when he knew it of the centurion, he [Pilate] gave the body to Joseph' (Mark 15:45). The centurion had come to realize that Christ had died not as a criminal but as a Saviour.

He had others with him who also believed. '. . . and they that were with him . . . feared greatly, saying, Truly this man was the Son of God' (Matt. 27:54). What a miracle of God's grace that some of the men who nailed the Lord Jesus to the cross and had earlier mocked Him, now confessed His deity: 'Whosoever believeth that Jesus is the Christ is born of God' (1 John 5:1).

The miracle in the sky

All three writers of the synoptic Gospels record that at Calvary darkness covered the whole land from the sixth until the ninth hour (Matthew 27:45; Mark 15:33; Luke 23:44-45).

At the birth of Christ, the glory of the Lord shone round about the shepherds (Luke 2:9). In contrast, at His death God draped the land in a supernatural darkness. The event cannot be explained by an eclipse of the sun, as it was Passover, the time of the full moon. God Himself, the great Creator, alone controls the movements of the sun. 'He maketh his sun to rise . . .' (Matt. 5:45); not merely controlled by a law of nature, but commanded daily by the Lord.

Job was asked by the Lord, 'Hast thou commanded the morning . . . and caused the dayspring . . . ?' (38:12).

Luke uses the verb *darkened* (23:45). This was an act of God Himself: the same God in whose name Joshua commanded the sun to stand still (Josh 10:13).

The prophet Amos spoke of a day of judgment that is still future; but, doubtless, his words can be applied to the darkness that surrounded the cross. 'And it shall come to pass in that day, saith the Lord God, that I will cause the sun to go down at noon, and I will darken the earth in the clear day; and I will make it as the mourning of an only son . . .' (Amos 8:9-10). We remind our hearts that the One who was impaled on the cross and suffered in the darkness was God's only Son.

When the Law was given at Mount Sinai, it was a scene shrouded in darkness: 'And the people stood afar off, and Moses drew near unto the thick darkness where God was' (Exod.

20:21). In the darkness of Calvary, Christ became answerable for a broken law and the full penalty was exacted from Him. The darkness that enveloped the cross intensified the aloneness of the man on the centre cross: 'Lover and friend hast thou put far from me, and mine acquaintance into darkness' (Ps. 88:18).

Morally, the world is a world of darkness, as Isaiah stated: 'For, behold, the darkness shall cover the earth, and gross darkness the people . . .' (60:2). The Christian's goal in this world is 'that ye should shew forth the praises [virtues] of him who hath called you out of darkness into his marvellous light' (1 Pet. 2:9).

It is true that the miracle of the darkened sky was from the sixth until the ninth hour. At the ninth hour, when the Lord Jesus bowed His head and dismissed His Spirit, light once again broke through where for three hours all had been darkness.

> *Darkness hung around Thy head,*
> *When for sin Thy blood was shed,*
> *Victim in the sinner's stead:*
> *Saviour, we adore thee.*
>
> S. Trevor Francis

The Ninth Hour

The ninth hour is mentioned by three Gospel writers (Matt. 27:45; Mark 15:33; Luke 23:44). It was the most significant moment in the world's history.

It was then that:

Calvary's Victor cried, 'It is finished' (John 19:30)

He bowed His head and dismissed His spirit (Matt. 27:50; John 19:30)

The veil was rent, the earth did quake, the rocks rent (Matt. 27:51)

The graves were opened (v. 52)

The Centurion believed (v. 54)

The darkness, which had enveloped the whole land for three hours, was dispelled (v. 45)

Hallelujah, what a Saviour.